ENGLISH-SPANISH TRANSLATION, THROUGH A CROSS-CULTURAL INTERPRETATION APPROACH

Francisco Castro-Paniagua

University Press of America, ® Inc.
Lanham • New York • Oxford

Copyright © 2000 by
University Press of America, ® Inc.
4720 Boston Way
Lanham, Maryland 20706

12 Hid's Copse Rd.
Cumnor Hill, Oxford OX2 9JJ

Library of Congress Cataloging-in-Publication Data

Castro-Paniagua, Francisco.
English-Spanish translation, through a cross-cultural interpretation
approach / Francisco Castro-Paniagua.
p.cm.
Includes bibliographical references and index.
1.   English language—Translating into Spanish.   2.   Translating and
interpreting—English-speaking countries.   3. Language and culture—
English-speaking countries.   4. Translating and interpreting—Latin
America.   5. Spanish language—Translating into English.
6.   Translating and interpreting—Spain.   7. Language and culture—
Latin America.   8. Language and culture—Spain.   I. Title.
PE1498.2.S65 C37   2000   468'.0221—dc21   00-036402 CIP

ISBN 0-7618-1711-5 (cloth: alk. ppr)
ISBN 0-7618-1712-3 (pbk: alk. ppr.)

⊖™ The paper used in this publication meets the minimum
requirements of American National Standard for Information
Sciences—Permanence of Paper for Printed Library Materials,
ANSI Z39.48—1984

I dedicate this work to my parents,
Gracia Paniagua de Castro and José Castro
Alférez, from whom I learned a sense of good
will, who have always wanted the best for me,
and who have tried to teach me the wisdom and
value of life.

Contents

Preface

————————————————————————————

Translation is a discipline that involves not only technical and structural transpositions from one language to another, but it is also tied to several other areas of human knowledge as anthropology, sociology, linguistics, psychology, history, and geography. Translation's realm is not only concerned with the universal study of humanity but it also dwells as well on the differences between human beings, since its essence is that of symbolizing a bridge that conects distinctive visions of the world. An exclusive knowledge of the mechanical side of translation will only render a partial picture of a given message across languages. In the particular case of English and Spanish translation we find two contrasting cultural paths, which are not totally opposed but that possess enough areas of discrepancy to represent a problem to the individual who wishes to convey messages from one linguistic code to another.

To begin my study I talk about the reasons and causes behind people's differences and how we can get around them to achieve a better understanding of each other's ways. Some of the people whose ideas I apply to translation are Dell Hymes, Franz Boas, Claude Lévi-Strauss, and Octavio Paz. Then I more specifically discuss Anglo-Saxon and Hispanic societies and I arrive at the conclusion that there are basic traits from which many of the elements that shape both cultures arise. I acknowledge the drive towards independence of the Anglo-Saxon character and the opposite impulse towards dependence of the Hispanic personality. I mention the Anglo-Saxon culture's tendency to control and dominate the environment and the Hispanic propensity towards contemplation of and identification with nature. I choose literary works that contain examples of cultural issues to prove that translators must be able to perceive and acknowledge his own and different cultural perspectives in order to transmit any given message across languages. To provide an empirical dimension to the study I analyze two different published translations of well known literary works to try to determine which translators made the proper decisions in regards to cultural considerations.

ACKNOWLEDGEMENTS

The author wishes to express appreciation to the following authors, and publishers for granting permission to quote from their materials in this book:

1.- Excerpts from "La Casa de Bernarda Alba", "La Casada Infiel", and "Romance Sonámbulo" by Federico García Lorca (Obras Completas, Galaxia Gutenberg, 1996 edition) ©Herederos de Federico García Lorca. English-language translation or "La Casada Infiel" by Ilsa Barea. © Ilsa Barea and Herederos de Federico García Lorca. All rights reserved. For information regarding rights and permissions for works by Federico García Lorca, please contact William Peter Kosmas, Esq., 8 Franklin Square, London W14 9UU, England.

2.- Agencia Literaria Carmen Balcells, S. A., Barcelona, Spain for lines from the poem "No es necesario" in its entirety and lines from "Por fin no hay nadie", from *Memorial de la Isla Negra* by Pablo Neruda.

3.- Grove/Atlantic, Inc. for eight lines from: Borges, Jorge Luis. *A Personal Anthology*, Trans. Anthony Kerrigan. New York: Grove Press, Inc. 1967.

4.- Grove/Atlantic, Inc. for A New Decade (Poems: 1958-1967) by Pablo Neruda; 11 lines from "Inthe End There is Nobody" and 28 lines from "No one Need Whistle" both translated by Ben Belitt. Copyright 1969 by Ben Belitt.

5.- Simon & Schuster, for excerpts totalling 23 lines from *The Old Man and the Sea* by Ernest Hemingway. © 1952 by Ernest Hemingway.

6.- Fondo de Cultura Económica for excerpts from *El Laberinto de la Soledad* by Octavio Paz; as well as material from *Pedro Páramo* by Juan Rulfo; both works copyrighted by Fondo de Cultura Económica, Carr. Picacho Ajusco NO. 227, Col Bosques del Pedgregal, Deleg. Tlalpan, 14200 México, D. F. (I am especially grateful to the late Don Octavio Paz for personally agreeing to the inclusion of these quotes without any monetary fee; as well as the Rulfo family estate for the same consideration).

7.- Editorial Porrúa, S. A., Av. Rep. Argentina No. 15 Altos, Apartado Postal M-7990, Admon. 1; 06020 México, D.F. Excerpts from *El Retrato de Dorian Gray*, original by Oscar Wilde, trans. by Monserrat Alfau; and *Tom Sawye,* original by Mark Twain, trans. by Arturo Soto.

8.- Barbara Flores Dederick for the translations "Faithless Wife" (original entitled *La Casada Infiel* by Federico García Lorca); and "Rocking" (original entitled *Meciendo* by Gabriela Mistral).

9.- Penguin Putnam, Inc. for excerpts from "The Dead Man" by Jorge Luis Borges, from BORGES: A READER by Emir Rodriguez Monegal and Alistair Reid. Copyright ©1981 by Jorge Luis Borges, Alistair Reid, Emir Rodriguez Monegal. Used by permission of Dutton, a division of Penguin Putnam, Inc.

10.- Editores Mexicanos Unidos, S. A. Luis González Obregón NO. 5, México 1, D. F. A.P. 45671, C.P. 06020, for excerpts from *El Retrato de Dorian Gray* original by Oscar Wilde, trans. by Ettore Perri; and *Tom Sawyer* original by Mark Twain, trans. by Federico Patán.

11.- Farrar, Straus & Giroux, Inc. for excerpts from "At Last There Is No One," "It Is Not Necessary" from ISLA NEGRA by Pablo Neruda. Translation copyright © 1981 by Alistair Reid. Reprinted by permission of Farrar, Straus & Giroux, Inc.

12.- Joan Daves Agency for the poem Meciendo by Gabriela Mistral and its translation "Rocking" by Doris Dana from SELECTED POEMS OF GABRIELA MISTRAL. Reprinted by arrangement with Doris Dana, c/o Joan Daves Agency as agent for the proprietor. Copyright © 1971 by Doris Dana.

13.- I would like to thank my cousins Rosa María Díaz de Rolón and Javier Paniagua Díaz for their invaluable help in obtaining on my behalf permissions from several of the publishing houses in Mexico.

Chapter I

The Prospectus

The importance of cross-cultural considerations upon undertaking a translation task has been acknowledged by several specialists in the field, as stated by Eugene Nida (1964) in *Toward a Science of Translation*. Justin O'Brien (1959) said the translator should possess a cultural background similar to that of the author, and if that is not the case, the translator should strive to compensate for that shortcoming. Nabokov (1941), Tytler (1790) and A. J. Arberry (1946) also approached the problem. But it is probably Eugene Nida who deals most directly with the cross-cultural aspect of translation. Nida warns of the danger of subjectivity in translating which has a wide application to the issue of cross-cultural considerations. The author says that it is almost inevitable that translators be affected by their own personal set of values, but they should attempt firmly to avoid any interference from their particular cultural background. I myself will base my analysis of cross-cultural considerations of English-Spanish translation on these principles as stated by Nida (1964).

Language is the reflection of a culture. Therefore, when transalting, one makes a cross-cultural comparison through a linguistic filter. Translation then has (besides all the different functions of communicating information) an inherent characteristic of cross-cultural comparison. When translating one compares languages, cultures and societies. Octavio Paz says in his essay *Traducción: Literatura y Literalidad* (1971) that when one hears the sounds of another language for the first time, the spectrum of emotions that one experiences goes from incredulity to outrage, and from horror to doubt about one's own language (p.7). Even though Paz is referring to languages, the same might very well apply to cultures and societies. Comparing different perceptions of the world frequently becomes a painful experience, especially while reflecting and analyzing one's own society; and one discovers areas that one would prefer to think of as nonexistent in the cultural embodiment.

Cultural features that might be considered ideal in one society may represent negative traits in another. Because of this, impartiality and objectivity may be difficult to achieve. Franz Boas and Lévi-Strauss present a series of reasons which seek to explain the origins of cultural ethnocentricity. I will deal with them in detail. Dell Hymes is also concerned with the problem of objectivity in his studies on ethnography. Hymes (1980) says in "What is Ethnography?" that one should acknowledge all cultural traits in embarking on the ethnographical analysis of a foreign society, even if one does not personally agree with those traits (p.96). However, the same may apply to the perception of one's own culture. Here, the problem will not lie in accepting new and different visions of the world, but in being able to recognize and accept the existence of negative traits, side by side with all the excellent characteristics we are more eager to identify in our culture.

Following Dell Hymes' (1980) cultural approach, translators should try to perform an ethnographical appraisal of the topic in which they will be working. If they are conducting a literary translation, the first step is to become familiar with the subject or various subjects with which the literary work deals. After they have isolated the cultural framework in which the plot unfolds, they should gather material on the subject. It is always a good idea to conduct this research from a wide variety of perspectives. That is, translators should try sociological, anthropological, psychological and other approaches. In addition to the technical abilities, they ought to develop an acute sense of cultural perception, as we have said before, and thus be able to analyze correctly the ethnography of a given literary work.

In the past, translators would typically give a rendition of their particular ethnographical perception of literary texts. This led to translators becoming well known literary figures themselves. Their fame was well deserved because of the importance of the work they performed, but the objectivity of their translations was sacrificied on the altar of their personal style and their own insight into the culture with which they were dealing. Translators must not only have a better understanding of the scientific methods of translation but must also have an open-mindedness towards the society in which their work is involved. Since valid ethnographic data largely depends upon efficiency and talent through perception and imagination rather than upon affinity or identification (Hymes 1980, p.96) translators must not only be able to grasp another cultural outlook (even if they do not agree with it), but must also be able to accept aspects of their own culture which they personally find hard to accept or are reluctant to admit.

Therefore, performing an ethnographical appraisal means making an incursion into areas that may jolt one's cultural sensitivity and place translators face to face with aspects of their society that they would prefer remain unexamined. However, if the translators' job is to produce a work that is recognized and appreciated in all its value and importance they must assume the responsibility for recognizing their own cultural reality.

It can be seen how the task of translation extends to several areas, and a translator has to assume the roles of historian, psychologist, sociologist, etc., in addition to the more obvious roles of semanticist, polyglot, linguist, etc.

Translation can be a pharmacon because it can both edify and destroy. It can edify if we are truly objective and impartial. It can destroy if we let ourselves be overcome by rage as Paz (1971) has also said (p.7), because once we find ourselves in such mental state, subconsciously or deliberately we will tamper with messages we are supposed

to convey. Throughout history we can find examples of the
consequences brought upon by such blindness. When
Spaniards saw the New World for the first time they
perceived it through their own cultural filter and that impelled
them to destroy it, since they "translated" it to their own
cultural framework and obviously many aspects of the
Indian's civilization did not fit within their vision of the
universe. Another well known example is the Bible, which
has undergone countless translations through more than five
thousand years. All that filtering must have altered
significantly the original texts which crossed over so many
cultures, historical periods, and different social
environments. If we reflect about this for a second, we
realize that the repercussions are enormous. As every
culture, epoch, and society interprets in its own way the
contents of such a transcendental text as the Bible --
fundamental at least to Western Civilization--, its contents
may have been distorted through the centuries, sometimes
probably at the whim of leaders of institutions and societies,
who saw a way to make it conform to their purposes
whether political, social or other.

Authors of an original text may not be capable of
understanding another culture that is different from their
own, but translators must necessarily have the capacity to
perceive more than just their own society. The absence of
this quality results in misunderstandings that can have either
relatively minor consequences or very serious ones,
depending on the level at which the translation is taking
place. Arriving at a full understanding of another way of life
that is different from our own involves great difficulties and
challenges as Hymes (1980:92) points out. Human beings
find alien ways hard to accept and comprehend. But there
have always been those who have tried to find paths for
societies to understand each other. Their ideas can be of
great help to those who are dedicated to communication
tasks, like translation. Some of the fields of human
knowledge that deal with the study of culture are sociology,
anthropology, linguistics, philosophy, literature, etc. Many
of the great minds of our times and our history belong to
these disciplines. Some of the people whose ideas we will

try to apply to translation will be Dell Hymes, Franz Boas, Claude Lévi-Strauss and Octavio Paz.

Lévi-Strauss (1975) says that perhaps the greatest obstacle towards achieving and understanding of another culture is our own denial of foreign idiosyncrasies and our fear to acknowledge them (p.100). There is a natural dread of losing our identity, and it seems that the recognition of the existence of other cultural ways makes us feel that we are somehow being swallowed into a new entity. Thus, we either disapprove of them or deny their presence. But if we are willing to accept other ways of life, there is also a fine line between objectively discerning one another's societies and becoming judgemental over cultural differences. As Hymes (1980:92) has noted, we must try to maintain a clear definition of that fine line. The subtlety required for this task demonstrates the transcendence of a discipline which has to do with distinctive cultures, like translation. An exclusive knowledge of the mechanical side of translation will only render a partial picture of a given message across languages. In the particular case of English and Spanish translation we find contrasting cultural paths, which are not totally opposed but which possess areas of discrepancy significant enough to represent a problem to the individual who wishes to convey messages from one linguistic code to another.

To begin the study I will discuss the reasons and causes behind human differences and how we could get around them to achieve a better understanding of each other's ways. Then I will discuss more specifically Hispanic and Anglo-Saxon societies. I will analize the drive towards independence and self-reliance in the Anglo-Saxon character and the opposite impulse towards dependence of Hispanic personality. I will deal with the tendency in Anglo-Saxon culture to control and dominate the environment and the Hispanic propensity towards contemplation and identification with nature. Analyses of specific literary works will provide examples which demonstrate sharpness of cultural perception to be an essential requirement for a good translation. Finally, using the theory of Propositional

Analysis developed by Mildred Larson in *Meaning-Based Translation* (1984) I will compare published translations of other well-known literary works, as I attempt to detect correct and erroneous cultural interpretations in regards to decisions made by the translator.

Chapter II

Review of the Literature

A. Culture

In this chapter I will present an overview of anthropological theories which deal with the universal notions that characterize most social systems that we denominate by the name of culture. I posit the need to mention these concepts because there are basic assumptions that lie underneath the structure of every culture. For this purpose, I will present the ideas of Franz Boas, Claude Lévi-Strauss and Dell Hymes. After reviewing several theories of the general concept of culture I will focus on the specific cases of Anglo-Saxon and Hispanic cultures and will make up a list of basic characteristics the understanding of which has special importance for translation to successfully convey cultural information from one language to another. I will resort to cultural analyses of Anglo-Saxon culture by Hsu and Williams, as well as the ideas of Paz on Hispanic culture. In the last part of the chapter I will review how different theories of translation refer one way or another to the importance of the cultural aspect of such a discipline.

Men have often attempted to reinforce the differences among them, reinforcements motivated by a need for identity and meaning in the total context of the universe.

This phenomenon takes place at all levels of society: individual, kinship, national, and ethnic. Claims of differentiation manifest themselves in various forms: physical, mental, or cultural. The human side which strives for understanding and communication among all individuals has been gradually reconciling the differences that we impose on each other.

Several questions necessarily artise when dealing with human differentiation. Controversies as old as humankind itself appear when different visions of the world are analyzed, but must be dealt with in order for different social communities to understand and communicate among each other.

The task is worthwhile if one believes what Octavio Paz said about different perspectives of the universe. They should not alienate us but rather complement one another. We may never succeed in determining when people first began assigning different signs to the surrounding environment, because it is not known if our present stage of cerebral evolution occurred in only one area of the planet or in several places at the same time. The fact is that all human beings, regardless of race, possess the same brain capacity to perceive the outside world. However, it is undeniable that each of us gives different accounts of his/her experiences of that world.

1.- *Franz Boas*

Even though Geroge W. Stocking (1968) states in his book *Race, Culture and Evolution* that Franz Boas did not have a systematic theory of culture, he agrees that many anthropologists "who in turn developed more systematic cultural theories" were disciples of Boas and considered him the founder of the anthropological study of culture (p.196). However, from a philosophical point of view, if not from the perspective of a patterning of cultural phenomena, Boas represents perhaps the earliest attempt to conceive a theory of culture truly devoid of prejudice and subjectivity (p.198). Before 1900, both the German and

Anglo-American traditions considered culture to be a successive acquisition of the manifestations of human endeavors such as art, science, and knowledge, enterprises that would liberate humans from natural and environmental bondage (p. 201). In this sense, culture did not mean tradition, and it was not considered to determine behavior, which was placed more in the realm of instinct and identified with an inferior evolutionary stage, usually referred to in racial terms (p.202).

It seems that Boas developed his concept of culture by gradually departing from the existing theories. He was probably one of the first anthropologists to regard culture as present in all human communities, although not in the same degree, but at a higher or a lower level. However, Boas was the first anthropologist to use culture as a pluralistic phenomenon. Before him, anthropologists would talk of "cultural stages", or "forms of culture" but not of cultures (p.203). Stocking (1968) mentions that it was Boas' fieldwork and interaction with the groups he studied, such as the northwestern North American Indians, which made him appreciate their culture and mentality (p.204).

When Boas was working on the Northwest Coast he realized that tribes which had different languages shared similar myths and beliefs, and that tribes with the same language presented distinctive mythologies. This caused him to conclude that some of the aspects of the cultures of these tribes were original while others were borrowed (p.206). This represents the same line of thought followed by Lévi-Strauss decades later in regards to the coalition of cultures which are nurtured by the contributions made among each other. Boas also realized that there was a difference between evolutionary biology and evolutionary ethnology. According to the theory of uniform evolutionary sequence among forms of culture, societies find themselves into one single line of cultural development. In other words, the idea that some societies are superior to others, while those which are inferior follow behind and strive to overtake the more advanced forms. Boas on the other hand, believed that ideas can appear independently in separate communities or individuals, a notion that pointed towards the theory of culture developing in differrent directions (p. 208).

Near the end of the ninetheenth century, the two main trends in anthropology were the historical method and the new theory of diffusion. The historical method featured "the single line of development" concept, and the theory of diffusion proposed that similarities found in the history of neighboring societies were the result of cultural spreading. The historical method tried to explain those similarities in terms of different stages along the same line of development and therefore the presupposition of superior and inferior cultures. As early as the time when Boas was developing his critique of evolutionism, we can see (as mentioned by Stocking) that the setting of the idea "the genius of one single people" could not take credit for the build up of the early civilizations of mankind. Instead Boas posited that the idea of dissemination was gaining momentum, through numerous proofs of contact between people and through the premise that this diffusion could not be prevented by any obstacle of language, race, or distance. Boas was an advocate of the idea that historical events had a determinant role in the course which races would follow to arrive to a certain form of civilization. He began to sketch the concept that achievements of races were not an indicator that one race was more gifted than another (p.213).

Nevertheless, Boas maintained a duality in his concept of culture, as a result of the earlier anthropological doctrines on the subject matter. He did not agree, however, as we have seen, with the idea that tribal mythologies were organic outgrowths from other cultures. Instead, he thought, those cosmogonies had acquired foreign material from other cultural sources and adopted and changed it in accordance with the genius of their people. Since this was the time of conceptual changes in anthropology, expressions like "the genius of the people" were misused exactly in the opposite from the way Boas had intended (p.214). In other words, the concept was interpreted by some as reminiscent of nineteenth century racial thought. On this issue, Boas also was ahead of its time when he wrote in 1911 *The Mind of Primitive Man*, in which he emphasized, along with the historical conditions of diffusion, the limitations met by criteria of evaluation upon the judgement of racial achievements. He also pointed towards the environmental agents theory as determinant of the physical similarities or differences among ethnic groups. This way, he was a precursor of the genetic theories that later developed (p. 215).

Although Boas was definitely avant-garde in his concepts, anthropological theory was not fully developed at that time, so he sometimes resorted to whatever opinions he had at hand. For instance he accepted as a validated opinion the theory of cessation of growth in the cerebral cortices of the lower races at adolescence. This assumption failed to realize that any given educational system is culturally conditioned and therefore will not instill the same kind of performance from students belonging to various cultural backgrounds. At any rate, Boas's interest in finding an appropriate answer to this issue caused him to suggest the school as a perfect place for the investigation of numerous individuals of different ethnic groups who live under similar circumstances (p. 215).

Boas began to realize that the best way to understand the culture of a given people was studying their folklore. Through his research with Northwest Coast Indians and in his arguments against mental differences based on racial assumptions, Boas came to the conclusion that dark-skinned people possessed the same traits of abstraction, inhibition and choice as the white-skinned Europeans, but that patterns of behavior were determined by the system of traditions in which every social group lives. Boas became aware that folklore embodies the values of a culture. Folklore contains whatever is good and bad, beautiful and ugly, etc. The genius of each people is comprised within their mythology as well as their "whole concept of the world." Boas also began to see as products of folklore cultures considered more civilized, in the sense that authority, tradition and habit all affect the idiosyncrasies of human beings in all forms of culture (p.220-226).

In contraposition with the Spencerian model which assumed that all cultural phenomena moved towards higher degree of complexity, Boas discovered that many primitive languages were far more complicated than English or Latin, and that some primitive music required the skilled of a virtuoso to be performed. Boas, glimpsing at the theories that would later be perfected by Lévi-Strauss, stated that it was only in historic or industrial development that Spencerian thought was fulfilled, however he attributed the fact to the idea that human tasks that do not depend on reasoning do not present the same type of development. Upon criticizing evolutionism Boas arrived to the conclusion that culture does not lead to a single sphere of human cognition, and before the refinement achieved by Lévi-Strauss on the matter, Boas declared that each culture was a unique way of life which was as valid as "our own" even if it was based on other traditions and different "equilibrium of emotion and reason" (p.227-228).

With which will later be echoed by Octavio Paz (1971), Boas described the universe as a continuous change of form and color in which every instant is determined by the previous moment and determines changes which follow. He realized that this truth of the universe could be clouded by our own subjectivity which compels us to assign a higher value to the cultural system that is "near and dear to us." When judging other cultures, our own cultural tradition makes us determine what is rational and what is not, based solely on the difference or sameness in regards to our perspective. According to Boas, the fact that we were born in a particular society which controls our every single thought, makes it very unlikely for us to see merit in any civilization other than our own and prevents us from wholly recognizing the assets of foreign cultures, simply because our lives have not unfolded under their dominance (p.229).

Boas was an advocate of relativism in anthropology in the sense that he posited that anthropologists should empty themselves of all personal judgements that would spring from any external canon in order to make a correct appraisal and interpretation. Boas extrapolated his important anthropological concept from already existing nomenclature such as historicity, plurality, behavioral determinism, integration, relativism, etc., but he gave new meaning to all these terms, uprooting them from a background of racial prejudice into a new light of cultural relativism. His work represented the transition between nineteenth and twentieth century anthropology. Thus, the legacy of Boas to anthropology resides most importantly in the redefinition he made of the existing theories and concepts. Although his use of some of those concepts was not consistent. According to Stocking (1968), for example, Boas employed the term "culture" in several antagonistic contexts and it appeared as if he did not have a clear picture of how he wanted to delimit the concept. This seems natural since he constituted the bridge between two lines of thought. Stocking says that Boas saw in the process of human culture the values that were part of his own personal perspective of the world: reason, freedom and human fellowship. He was a pioneer in recognizing the concept of cultural plurality which greatly facilitated the turning point in the way humankind viewed itself. He rejected the models of biological or racial determinism and ethnocentric criterion for a model of cultural appraisal. Likewise, he highlighted the influence of subconscious cultural processes in the particular expression of human behavior. He changed the abstraction of human beings from "rational" to "rationalizing", broadening at the same time the boundaries of the meaning of the term "rational" (p. 232).

2.- *Claude Lévi-Strauss*

Claude Lévi-Strauss (1975) in *Race and History* states that the development of distinctive human cultures is a "parallel phenomenon in a different sphere" (p.96). However, if human races originate in a common genetic pool, how can we account for the differente 'stages' of intellectual evolution that human cultures seem to present? This question would be irrelevant if it were not for the problems already mentioned that have arisen throughout history concerning the right of particular ethnic groups to dominate others 'less intellectually gifted'. For our purpose, the importance of the issue lies in its bearing on cultural communication and transcribability.

According to Lévi-Strauss, within the process of cultural activity there are some forces which accentuate particularism or diversity and others that foment covergence and affinity (p.98). An example of the former would be the differentiation of the Romance languages after the fall of the Roman Empire, and an example of the latter would be the effect of mass media on the different dialects of Spanish. However, the diversity of cultures depends more upon the interactions among them than it does upon their isolation (p. 99).

Human beings have always been prone to regard diversity as abnormal and outrageous, thus tending to reaffirm their distinctiveness from others (p.100). All human beings are inclined to reject anything that does not identify with themselves. Lévi-Strauss refers to expressions such as 'barbarous habits', 'not what we do', 'ought not to be allowed', as example of reactions to foreign ways of life. This way the Greeks called *barbarian* anything not included in their culture, and western civilization has used the term 'savage' the same way. Therefore, anything which does not accomodate to our society is deprived of cultural status and is confined to the domain of nature. Lévi-Strauss points out that it is precisely this attitude which is the most salient trait of the beings we call savages. The status of humanity is only granted to those belonging to the tribe, mirroring those who in turn label them savages. There are numerous examples of tribal communities who call themselves 'the men', 'the good', 'the escellent', 'the well-achieved', while one outside the tribe will be 'bad', 'wicked', 'ground-monkeys', or 'lousy eggs'. Sometimes the foreigners are denied the attribute of existence and they are called 'ghosts' or 'apparitions'. Lévi-Strauss mentions how after Spain had discovered America it sent commissions to investigate if Caribbean Indians had a soul, and the Indians meanwhile were drowning white prisoners to investigate whether their bodies would decompose (p. 101).

In this way, by believing in 'barbarism' we become barbarian ourselves. In order to account for customs that are displeasing or to refute cultural variations which are incomprehensible to its personal idiosyncrasies, contemporaneous humankind has devised a sort of false evolutionism. According to this line of thought all human cultures find themselves in a lineal succession of development, with some of them at a more advanced stage of evolution and others at a lower level of sophistication (p.102).

One of the greatest sins committed by cultural research has been to gather the few aspects that time has left us of a long-disappeared social system and compare them to contemporary civilization, expecting them to conform to each other in every aspect, simply because both present apparent similarities (p.104).

For instance, since certain tribes practice hunting rituals, we suppose that prehistoric paintings must also have constituted hunting rites. And since from our point of view those practices have no pragmatic purpose, we conclude that prehistoric etchings likewise had no practical use (p.105). Western civilization in particular tends to see cultures of the rest of the world as parallel to its own line of development, but at earlier periods, depending on the technological advance of the specific culture. However, all human societies have a history of equal extension in time. At first glance, it seems logical to think that while some communities were always accumulating knowledge and discoveries, others lacked the talent of synthesis. But this may be an oversimplification (p.107).

Until recently, it was thought that prehistoric man had followed a certain line in developing tools. We are now discovering that methods of chipping and polishing stone, which once were considered to be successive stages, were in reality practiced at the same time (p.108). We now have to redifine our concept of progress from a sense that some societies journey through it at a faster rhythm, while others lag at a snail's pace to a view that progress takes different routes, that it leaps, that it bounds, but not always in the same direction. Lévi-Strauss compares the movement of progress to the different pieces on a chess board (p.109). Human progress can not be equated to climbing the steps of a ladder; it is more like the tossing of the dice, only occasionally the numbers add up to a lucky combination, but the game takes thousands of years and we lose the right perspective of how it takes place.

Different cultures follow different progress paths. But progress in distinctive areas have only a relative meaning to our own way of life. Thus, cultures that have contributed and affected our cumulative civilization, will seem to have made more progress. We consider others stationary because we can not measure their line of development in terms of the criterion of our own culture (p.111). Therefore, the significance of the history of a society depends not on its inherent values but in the relationship it bears to our own way of perceiving the world and or own interests. All through our lives we aree costantly bombarded by thousands of pieces of information which will influence and program our ability to judge our own civilization and the civilizations around us. We carry this system within ourselves everywhere we go and we will evaluate cultural manifestations through this filter imposed by our own cultural blueprint. The meaning of another culture will be contingent upon the amount of information our cultural program allows us to process and our capability of shifting the focus to which we are accustomed. If we are unable to adjust that focus we will perceive other cultural manifestations as blurred or nonexistent. Lévi-Strauss describes this experience as being on board trains travelling in opposite directions. Depending on the speed our train is travelling, the other train loses its features and we are only able to determine a partial amount of information about the actual characteristics of the passing train. The faster the other train is travelling, the fewer traits we will be able to identify from our own moving perspective (p.112).

Therefore, our inability to perceive the actual interests of a given society may result in a false impression of immobility regarding that culture, and the same reaction can be expected from the participants of that community towards us. We usually call any society that has stayed behind in the constant evolution of technology in Western Civilization "underdeveloped" or "primitive." However, all those 'secondary' societies, even if we see them as uniformly backward, can be similar or totally opposite. Different perspectives will give different cultures dominance in diverse aspects of human progress (p.113).

Lévi-Strauss enumerates remarkable examples of such achievements: Eskimos as the human community which has overcome the harshest of physical environments; India as possessing the world's most elaborate philosophical and religious system; Islam as having triumphed during the Middle Ages over by then static European cultures on the interrelationship of all aspects of human life (technological, economic, social and spiritual); the Far East as being thousands of years ahead in regards to the link between body and mind. Even cultures which are in deep economic 'underdevelopment' like the Australian aborigines and the Melanesian, can still have the most complicated and harmonious system of familiar and social groups, and inspire the modern study of Social Science. The contributions of Egypt are well known (p.115). So are the sophistications of the Pre-Colombian cultures of America such as the Maya, the Incan and the Toltec, whose most important achievements are just beginning to unravel. The theological, psychological, and scientific legacies of Jewish culture to Western Civilization are another example of the highest human achievement.

Modern ethnology is currently more involved in discovering the originality of every society in its approach to solving problems, and the true motives for the choices made in each culture, than in the inventory of their accomplishments (p. 116). In the midst of all this theory there is still one undeniable fact: the westernization of the world. Is that not telling us that Western Civilization is superior to others? Several issues come into consideration in order to answer this question. First, Western Civilization is actually the culmination of ten thousand years of human civilization arising, not from a single cultural community but from several. Second, has Western Civilization always been readily accepted, or has it been superimposed, at least in certain cases? Third, has that imposition been the product of cultural or physical superiority? (Pre-Colombian American cultures were physically overpowered by a culture that was behind them in several areas of science.) Fourth, are we witnessing a long lastig phenomenon (it has been taking place for only the last 150 years) or is it a cyclic process? (pp. 116-117).

Lévi-Strauss elaborates in depth the issue of human progress and concludes that whatever field of development and whichever path it has followed, the most refined products of such process are the transmission and improvements of techniques, generation after generation. Do certain societies have a higher ability to accumulate intellectual and technical achievements? How do we account for the instances in history in which there seems to be an unusual production of geniuses, like during the Renaissance? Again, we need to remember that it all depends on the kind of criteria we are using to appreciate these instances in history. Surely, there are other golden ages in other areas of cognition that are imperceptible to us, because they have no meaning to our own system of beliefs and interest. In addition, several societies arrive at thresholds that might point towards the same line of development and then shift course to another direction. Examples are the discovery of gun powder in China, where use did not go beyond the manufacturing of fireworks; and the acquaintance of Pre-Colombian Mexican culture with the wheel, which they only employed in the fabrication of toys. These two inventions are clearly turning points in the rise of technical societies (p. 124).

Cultures which follow different routes do not always move away from each other. Sometimes their particular achievements combine and blend into one single civilization and those are precisely the instances in which mankind reaches its maximum potential. Such was the case of Egypt, which amalgamated the advances of Asia and Africa, giving the world one of its most important civilizations to date. Cultures can amalgamate through various means: migration, borrowing, trade and warfare. Often times the alliances are not formed willingly and the receptor and contributing cultures may not be aware of the benefits both will gain from the union until much later in their history. Therefore, it is very difficult for any society to claim superiority since any culture cut off from foreign input, would become so alienated that it would be difficult to make any cumulative advances (p. 126).

Further, societies which praise themselves as being superior believe so in great part because their achievements hava a universal appeal. This really demonstrates that they have reached their stage of development through coalitions. In this way, Europe represents an alliance of cultures which gave way to the birth of Western Civilization. During the Renaissance, the European continent was the merging point of several cultural manifestations: Greek, Roman, Germanic, Anglo-Saxon, Jewish, Islamic and Chinese. Pre-Colombian America received cultural influences which were apparently less varied, giving the American continent a more uniform cultural profile. Lévi-Strauss believes this was probably the cause behind the Amerindian empires' defeat by the conquerors (p. 127). However, we are now discovering there were other factors like the mysterious awareness of ancient Americans of the existence of white people who whould one day arrive to their continent from the east, and the belief that they would come with a peaceful purpose, which aided the perpetration of the conquest.

The cumulative quality of any given culture represents more a behavior than an inherent characteristic. The real problem with any society would come about if such a community decided to isolate itself, since exterior contributions would be prevented from enriching its perception of the world. The greatest obstacle to the benefits of cultural contributions is the refusal of societies to renounce their own 'identity'. The key to benefiting from the cultural diversity among societies depends on the capability of each society to accept and understand other forms of cultural expression. This is one of the most problematic challenges mankind faces (p.128). Ironically, it is not restricted as we have seen to so-called primitive societies, but may be even more so to cultures which flatter themselves that they are more highly sophisticated. According to Lévi-Strauss, the phenomenon of cultural diversity and the consequent process of rejection and acceptance is only an inherent characteristic of the concept of 'world civilization', which constantly struggles between those two forces but compels mankind to renovate its legacy. He states that all cultures should consider the contributions of other people, not so much in terms of a list of inventions but in the differences each society offers up and in the validity of such differences, even if fundamental essence of any given differences escapes a particular mental frame (p. 129). A culture's open-mindedness is the secret to its further development. In the deterioration of such a quality lies the danger of a given community to interrupt valuable external input necessary to the continuity of human evolution.

Lévi-Strauss also points out there are risks presented by the cultural diversity of people, but the benefits brought about by cultural coalitions would still surmount these disadvantages. Social inequalities will very likely be present whenever different social manifestations are present. Exploitation will be another undesirable effect of cultural variation. Imperialism and colonialism have resulted in earlier times such as thenineteenth century from the import of foreign domination over a given society. There is no doubt however that humans must collaborate with each other if they aspire to progress in a wider range of disciplines (p.131). The dangers will always be present but they will be minor when compared to any kind of particularism and ethnocentricity which would threaten the dignity of cultural communities that might be little understood. At the same time, aiming at a monolithic way of life would fossilize mankind. Unification and diversity are two eternal forces that move mankind (p. 133). Awareness and understanding of diverse cultural phenomena are vital to a series of human enterprises destined to the better communication between human beings complementing each other.

3.- Dell Hymes

Dell Hymes broke important ground in the field of linguistic anthropology in general and ethnography in particular. In *What is Ethnography?* (1980 ed.) Hymes defines ethnography in its widest sense as the study of people and their way of life, their culture, their society, and institutions (p.89). The most important contribution of ethnography, and its greatest challenge as well, is the study of people other than one's own ethnic group. Because we must deal with cultures different from our own, several problems arise with respect to our adequate perception of them (p. 92).

Since ethnography is an integral part of the science of anthropology, its observation must be impartial and objective. But ethnography involves not only observation; participation is also essential. According to Dell Hymes the attempt to make participation and observation systematic has led to the conception of three distinctive kinds of ethnography: comprehensive, topic-oriented, or hypothesis-oriented (p.90)

Early exercises in ethnography were carried out by the first colonizers when they rendered accounts of the societies they encountered in the New World. They tried to document and interpret a very complete picture of a civilization, and that for Hymes, is why their work was comprehensive (p.89). Since in this period in history most of the world was unknown to Europe, literally everything had to be learned about all the new societies they encountered. Therefore, all those early ethnographic attempts sought to be comprehensive.

Ethnography can also be topic-oriented, that is, it can focus on one aspect of a given society. Hymes mentions ethnographic work on kinship terminologies as being exemplary of this topic-oriented type. This methodology contains three steps to follow in anthropological research, namely: a contrastive insight, a gathering of specific information, and a general interpretation. When the science of anthropology unites the three ingredients, it is making use of the ethnographical method (p.90).

Hymes claims ethnography becomes hypothesis-oriented when the anthropologist conceives a theoretical frame of a specific cultural topic and proceeds to make a comparison of contrasting societies through specific information (p.90).

When ehtnography has to deal with topics related to behaviors and institutions that are foreign to us, the aspect of *meaning* becomes essential to make the investigation valid. In such a situation, the risk of subjectivity exists, depending on the pariticular experience the researcher might have with the culture in question (p.93). A misunderstanding of this sort can lead to an invalid investigation. The key to validity in meaning is the awareness of diversity upon interpreting the features of a society. Besides the general vectors of age, sex, race, class, income, etc., meaning is drawn out form the very experiences encountered by the components of every society (p.94). Therefore, meanings change within every vision of the world. However, ethnography as a scientific mode of research cannot afford to fall prey to subjectivity. Here, Hymes stresses the importance of participation and observation to obtain valid conclusions, especially when meanings are implicit and have to be slowly discovered (p.95)

The structural interpretation of societies is essential to ethnography, but some socio-cultural aspects are not suitable for interpretation in structural terms. However, they may be more easily interpreted through presentation (p. 97). In this sense, narrative serves a function of presentation, according to Hymes, from which we perceive the mutual utility that binds ethnography and literature. As a matter of fact, in terms of correct interpretation of cultural frames, ethnography and literary acconts are reciprocally indispensable, as Dell Hymes points out (p.98).

Ethnographers are themselves the objects of their own inquiry, since they will perceive and interpret cultural facts through their own personal traits without avoiding some kind of partiality (p. 99). Actually, however, the particular talent of the ethnographer will make some information better stated and clarified. Thus, learning ethnographically does not necessarily undermine objectivity as might be suspected. To Hymes, ethnography requires a certain dose of trust and confidence in the ethnographer. After all, as Hymes says, every science imposes the same requirements of objectivity on its practitioners and eventually, if such accuracy is not met, all scientific research must be redefined in every field of human knowledge (p. 99).

Ethnography is the direct observation of cultural behavior in its natural context. Traditionally, this kind of investigation occurs in the area of cultural anthropology. However, ethnography does not have to be the exclusive tool of anthropological research. It can be applied to other disciplines as well, namely: sociology, semiotics, semantics, linguistics (more specifically to the realm of sociolinguistics), and to tasks that have to do with social groups and cultural manifestations. As regards to the issue of sociolinguistics, ethonography plays a role in finding out how a given society is linguistically stratified, according to its socio-cultural structures.

William Labov (1966) described in *The Social Stratification of English in New York City* the several dialectal variants of spoken English found in that city within the different ethnic groups that inhabit the metropolitan area. Labov showed that language varies its functions within the same code depending on the special socio-economic factors surrounding the speakers. He found out that within one community, groups that share a particular set of sociological traits, such as ethnic background, age, sex, occupation, economic status, etc., adopt a particular set of variants of the language.

In my opinion we can relate this issue to translation, the other discipline that represents our main concern. In fact, a translator should be an ethnographer the same way that a sociologist or a linguist is, because the translator has the responsibility of correctly interpreting, not only semantic information but the inherent cultural codes as well. And beyond interpreting, the translator must adequately transmit and adapt such message across cultures. Therefore, translators need to have a deep knowledge of the cultural frames they will be handling. Otherwise, translators will convey the erroneous cultural information. This does not mean that the translator will be held liable for an untranscribable cultural sign or a lack or universality in a given text. A work's potentiality to achieve universal dimensions will rest upon the literary genius of a writer. Thus, it is not the task of the translator to achieve such universality more than to transmit it, should it be intrinsic to the original text.

The translator's job is pretty much like the ethnographer's. Translators must become familiar with the concepts of a cultural community, instead of just finding a suitable equivalent to their own system of concepts. In the late fifties, an anthropological method based on relationships of language cognitive items started to develop. Based on this method, cognitive anthropologists believe that words label concepts and that by studying those words they can achieve a real understanding of the particular perspective.

Michael Agar (1974) establishes in *Ethnography and Cognition* that at the beginning of an ethnographical appraisal, the researcher will probably suffer from cultural shock (p. 3). He has to realize that such schock arises from a difference of cognition. The ethnographer must then find a way to reach an understanding of the new knowledge in order to be able to describe it. The first step to do this is to identify the signs which are the link to the specific body of knowledge pursued by the ethnographer (p. 4). The signs can be of several kinds, personal or contextual. Personal signs can be verbal or nonverbal and contextual signs can be divided into fashion and environmental. Likewise, verbal signs can be linguistic or paralinguistic, as classified by Azar. Afterwards, all these signs must be rearranged to give meaning to the pattern in which they occur (p. 7).

However, after identifying signs the ethnographer must be able to interpret them. This is not an easy task, because meanings do not often operate on a conscious level. Not all the members of a particular community are able to discuss their cultural signs with the same precision, and accounts of signs may vary from individual to individual. The most logical set of signs to look at first is language, according to Azar. But the cultural meanings of lexemes within a language also represent a wide range of difficulties. The first step in defining meanings is to group them in categories. After this, the ethnographer must observe the attributes and properties shared by all the members of such category or taxonomy. After categorization had been carried out, relationships among the different signs must be established. These classifications of signs aid the ethnographer in deciphering how cultural communities conceptualize the world (pp. 8-12).

In this way, we have seen that there are a number of basic assumptions that lie underneath the compostition of every culture, on of the most important being that most cultures conceive themselves as having traits that place them in a special position with reference to other societies. However, we have seen how important it is to rise above this concept in order to properly undersantd other cultural systems.

B.- Cross-cultural considerations.

The cultural framework in which the English and Spanish languages have developed followed substantially different historical paths. Those paths gave them a shape and a personality of their own with areas of contact and antagonistic aspects as well. Both languages share an Indo-European origin and their inception as well as a great part of their evolution took place in Western Europe. Other than during the period at the end of the Roman Empire and the French influence of the Middle Ages, however English and Spanish have taken very divergent routes.

Great Britain was originally populated, as far as we know, by Celtic groups indigenous to Northern European areas like Scandinavia, Germany and Spain, as stated by Ernest Barker in *The Character of England* (1947: 9-24). Eventually, subsequent migrations this time from Germany and Scandinavia formed the Anglo-Saxon ethnic group. These peoples left and indelible mark on the posterior culture of Great Britain. Although Germanic tribes also invaded Spain (the Visigoths), they left only a minor legacy to Iberian culture. The ethnic groups that most significantly influenced Spain were the Romans, the Arabs and the Jewish. Such predominance is evident in the language and the physical traits of the Spanish people. The physical environments in which these three comunities evolved also molded their character and their idiosyncracies. The north of Europe with its cold climate represented a hard test of survival for its dwellers. Such living conditions gave special characteristics to Northern Europeans. These people had to overcome the coldest of winters in Europe, which impelled them to device ways to supply themselves and their families with food and shelter.

Northern Europeans needed to develop their minds in a very practical manner to extract, from the hostile and greedy nature that surrounded them, their means of survival (p.463). The main priority to the inhabitants of this region became the conquest of the environment, in part through the conception of artifacts which later gave rise to the development of a technology that has reached the most sophisticated stages. These circumstances of evolution have made the emphasis on the material aspects of existence one of the most preponderant features of the Northern European mind. A series of consequences emerge form this perspective. One of the events in Anglo-Saxon history in which this existential trait is most evident can be identified at the core of the motives of why the English and Germanic Churches dissented and separated from the philosophical teachings of the Catholic Church of Rome (pp. 56-84). Protestantism and all its denominations exalt material progress as a sign of the acceptance of God (p. 325-326). This religious belief may reflect the attitude imposed on northern Europeans by a harsh environment in order for them to survive (p.4). In direct contrast, Latin culture, is profoundly rooted in the traditions of the Roman Catholic Church which preaches humility as one of the most desirable virtues in order to reach the favor of God. The wide acceptance of this philosophy throughout the Latin world has probably been achieved because these peoples have not had to face environments which demand material and physical protection for their survival, at least not as much as Northern Europeans. Because of these two reasons, Latin culture has not, in general praised the accumulation of material wealth but rather, the simplicity of living.

Therefore, the pursuit of technological and scientific advances leading to improve material existence was not emphasized in Mediterranean societies, except during the Renaissance during which all of Europe tried to free itself from the darkness of the Middle Ages which had been mainly perpetrated and perpetuated by the Catholic Church of Rome. Other than that period, Latin culture glorifies emotion over mind, aesthetics over pragmatism. Thus, the practice of art became the pinnacle of human intellect to the

Latin concept of life. These factors have constituted the foundation rocks for the rise of Anglo-Saxon and Latin cultures, and understanding them is crucial for accurate translation between English and Spanish.

As we have seen stated by Boas, Hymes and Lévi-Strauss, through the analyzing and comprehending the basic elements of cultures we can do a better job at accepting concepts that may apparently be alien and outrageous to our own way of conceiving reality. Octavio Paz is his essay *Translation: Literature and Literality* (1971) also applies that principle to the task of translation. He says that for more than two centuries philosophers, historians, anthropologists and linguists have realized the apparently unsurmountable differences between cultures, however those divergencies make cultures complement each other, providing a better picture of the universe (p.8).

Literature, as Hymes (1980) points out, is an important tool for ethnographic inquiry, and it is filled with narrative examples of cultural behavior (p.98). As an example of the basic features we have talked about so far in regards to the relative importance assigned to material progress by Anglo-Saxon and Latin societies we can mention the American novel *Gone With The Wind* by Margaret Mitchell (1936). There is a scene within the story when the main character Scarlett O'Hara pledges to herself upon losing her property to the ravages of Civil War (p. 428, 1964 ed.) that she will never be hungry again or let her family suffer privation. To the mind of the Latin reader this scene is bewildering to a certain degree, because it seems odd that the character's main priority be the material aspect, since the emotional plot had apparently been of foremost importance. All through the rest of the novel, Scarlett O'Hara's actions have as their main motivation the acquisition of material wealth over the fulfillment of her own emotions.

And touching upon the handling of emotions we arrive at another one of the most obvious contrasts between Anglo-Saxon and Latin cultures. The emphasis on physical survival reinforced by its Puritan background, to which we will refer later, has made Anglo-Saxon culture take a special approach to expressing feelings. Emotions are to be controlled and their display is considered undesirable. Latin culture on the contrary encourages the outlet of emotions, as a sign of humanity. There can be a clash of cultures on this subject when interaction between both ethnic groups takes place. From the Anglo-Saxon perspective, life can be handled more successfully when emotions are in control. Most affairs in life are aimed at staying in command and that goes hand in hand with material possession and everything related. Therefore, it is difficult to the Anglo-Saxon mind to conceive why Spanish-speaking countries have stayed so far behind in material progress and why Indians have accepted so 'passively' a fate of poverty and servitude through centuries.

1.- Hispanic Culture

As we stated earlier, several of the Iberian ethnic constituents are shared by the Anglo-Saxon group (Barker pp. 9-24). However, the path both cultures followed could not be more divergent, due to a number of historical and geographical reasons. In the first place, Spain received a much longer and far more overwhelming influence from the Roman Empire. In the second place, after the conclusion of the Roman influence, Spain was invaded by the Arabs, who stayed in the peninsula for over seven hundred years. This ethnic element gave Iberian culture a very distinctive personality, when compared with the rest of Euorpean societies. In the third place, a Sephardic Jewish community had existed in Spain even before the Muslims' arrival. After the discovery of America, this already complex ethnic group came into contact with the American Indian civilizations of the New Continent, as Emiliio Willems (1975) establishes in *Latin American Culture* (p.36).

This new racial ingredient removed Spanish culture even further apart from its European counterparts, not only idiosyncratically but also in physical appearance. And although we can talk about a separate Iberian culture, the demographic preponderance of the Latin American nations makes it all the more appropriate to talk about a general Spanish culture with related branches represented by the different ethnic groups that came to result after the colonization of America, as George M. Foster (1960: 2-6) points out in *Culture and Conquest*. In certain countries, as it is the case of Mexico, we can encounter the several levels of ethnic intermixing that resulted from the contact between Iberian and Indian groups. And all those shades of miscegenation are present in a higher or lower degree in all the other Hispanic countries. The same phenomenon occurred in the countries where there was a significant percentage of population of African origin. We can thus mention as the ethnic constituents of Latin America the Mestizo, the Indian, the Mulatto, the Black and the Caucasian. The largest group is possibly the Mestizo, although some countries, i.e., Argentina and Uruguay, have a larger Caucasian population in comparison with the Mestizo element. The importance of these classifications lies within the particular idiosyncratic characteristics of every group and how they have shaped what we call Latin American culture. There exists a large number of studies on the cultural nature of the Hispanic mind, but most of them refer to specific national traits of a particular area or country in Latin America. However, we have already said that we can find in all Latin American nations to a greater or lesser degree the basic groups that compose the ethinc picture from which Hispanic American culture resulted (Foster, 1960, p.2).

Even though Spain is the country where this culture originated, we can say that at this particular historical stage, the Iberian peninsula represents only a fraction of a more complicated ethnic identity (Foster, 1960, p.3). Therefore, a study dealing with the idiosyncratic traits of the Mestizo population of Mexico, for example, can very well apply to the other Latin American countries which include this ethnic element within their population. Likewise, an analysis of the characters of Spaniards will very closely apply to that sector of population in Latin American countries, meanig the full blooded Spaniards who most recently arrived to Hispanic America and who have not yet racially blended with the rest of the population. An investigation on the cultural features of a given Amerindian group will present most of the traits found in other American Indian societies (Foster, p.6). Naturally, there will be certain differences from group to group, but we can consider them part of the same ethnic trunk.

The clash of cultures that took place during the colonization of Spanish America followed a very similar process in all the centers of higher Indian civilization encountered by Spaniards. In some cases, like the Incan and the Aztec empires, there was considerable resistance against the conquistadors, but in general there was hardly an unconditional acceptance of the foreigners. As we have been recently discovering, some of these civilizations reached an extremely high stage of development, to the point that even modern science finds itself puzzled by advances made by these peoples which are nowadays still unmatched. However, the native American civilizations were too far behind their European counterparts as regards warfare and they were unable to confront their military apparatus. A significant part of the population was slain during the conquest and in some cases, as it is the case of the Caribbean Islands, the aborigines were virtually wiped out. The remaining Indians were subjected to slavery during the following three centuries (Worcester and Schaeffer, 1965, p.296).

Willems (1975) says miscegenation actually occurred in the Americas due to the fact that conquistadors came without women (p.35) which was a different situation from what happened in the British colonies where whole families actually came from Great Britain. At any rate, after some time there was a sector of the population that came to be known as *Mestizo*, part Spanish and part Indian. Even though they had Spanish blood, they were not considered Spanish and did not enjoy all the privileges that being Spanish implied. They were thought of as lighter Indians. Nevertheless, the Mestizo population grew faster than any other ethnic group in most of the countries of Latin America, especially after they gained their independence (p.37). Only in countries where the Indian population was reduced to an extremely small number, did the mestizo population not increase, as it is the case of Argentina and Uruguay. Otherwise, the Caucasian population became a minority. The same thing happened to the Indian population in most of the other Spanish American countries, either through racial mixing or extermination (p. 38). Because Mestizos are part Spanish and part Indian, it has been said that they embody the cultural conflict that resulted from the clash of Spanish and Indian societies. In that way, Mestizos experience love-rejection emotions towards their Spanish and Indian heritages. Their Spanish legacy makes them look up to Spain as the mother country and use the word *Indian* as an insult meaning primitive or stupid.

Octavio Paz

In Mexico, the Indian element makes Mexicans curse Spaniards as they shout a symbolic *¡Mueran los Gachupines!* on Independence Day celebrations, every year on the night of the fifteenth of September. Of course, this is in reference to Spaniards during the independence struggle at the beginning of the nineteenth century. Likewise Mestizos feel proud of the ancient civilizations of Pre-Colombian America. Thus, there are idiosyncratic contradictions and psychological ethnic conflicts found in a large sector of Latin American society, but they are of a very different nature from those that typify their Anglo-Saxon counterpart. This aspect of the Mestizo idiosyncracy results in a series of consequences that stem from the combination of these emotionally charged cultural forces. Such consequences are the elements that shape the character of Mestizos. The other segments of Spanish society also comprise the basic components of the Mestizo character but they do so in their pure essence before they were combined into a single group.

After the conquest and due to the treatment they received, the Indian population became distrustful and resentful, which repesented an appropriate response to a life of hardship and abuse. Ever since the discovery of America and up until Modern Anthropology began talking about the nonexistence from an evolutionary prespective, of primitive societies as such, Indian communities have been considered retrograde and underdeveloped. It has rarely been considered that the Indian character is the reaction of people who were subjugated and uprooted from their coltures and whose societies were destroyed.

As we have mentioned earlier, there are strong idiosyncratic parallelisms among most of the Spanish speaking countries. We can still discover the love-hate relationship among the different ethnic fractions of the population: the old presumption of European superiority hand-in-hand with the resentment caused by centuries of abuse; pride of Spanish ancestry and shame over the exploitation prepetrated against Indians; admiration of the ancient Indian civilizations mixed with pain over the destruction of those cultures. All of these interweaving emotions coexist within Hispanic society. They are opposing forces that had been hidden throughout five centuries.

Octavio Paz talks about *máscaras mexicanas* (Mexican masks) in *El Laberinto de la Soledad* (1980 ed.). These masks cover the true identity of Mexicans, according to Paz, who says:

> Viejo o adolescente, criollo o mestizo, general, obrero o licenciado, el mexicano se me aparece como un ser que se encierra y se preserva: máscara el rostro y máscara la sonrisa. (p. 26).

To Paz, the Mexican personality defends its intimate nature with silence and words; politeness and contempt: irony and resignation. He respects his neighbor's privacy as his own; he does not even dare to touch his neighbor with his eyes.

> Su lenguaje está lleno de reticencias, de figuras y alusiones, de puntos suspensivos; en su silencio hay repliegues, matices, nubarrones, arcoiris súbitos, amenazas indescifrables (p.26).

In the eyes of the Mexican character, to open up is a sign of weakness or an act of treachery. "El mexicano puede doblarse, humillarse, 'agacharse', pero no 'rajarse', esto es, permitir que el mundo penetre su intimidad." (p.26).

Octavio Paz says that Mexicans' impenetrability is just a resource of their distrust and suspicion. Manhood is measured by the invulnerability before any weapon or the impact of the outside world.

"El estoicismo es la más alta de nuestras virtudes guerreras y políticas. Nuestra historia está llena de frases y episodios que revelan la indiferencia de nuestros héroes andte el dolor o el peligro... Más que el brillo de la victoria nos conmueve la entereza ante la adversidad." (p.28)

Octavio Paz considers that the tendency of Mexicans to close in several of their existence: Their unalterable courtesy; the persistance of Classical Humanism, the fondness of closed forms of poetry, and the propensity towards formulas, whether social, moral or bureaucratic. The necessity to confine themselfes causes Mexicans to learn the art of dissimulation. Paz says:

Simular es inventar o, mejor, aparentar y así eludir nuestra condición. La disimulación exige mayor sutileza; el que disimula no representa, sino que quiere hacer invisible, pasar desapercibido -sin renunciar a ser-. El mexicano excede en el disimulo de sus pasiones y de sí mismo. Temeroso de la mirada ajena, se contrae, se reduce, se vuelve sombra y fantasma, eco. No camina, se deliza; no propone, insinúa; no replica, rezonga; no se queja, sonríe (p.38).

Octavio Paz points out that all these impulses to hide and dissimulate arose during the colony. It was the particular way Indians and Mestizo had to deal with their desires of rebellion against the Spaniards. The colony does not exist anymore but distrust and suspicion remain in the character of Mexicans (p.39). Actually it has become a cultural trait, and it has invaded other aspects of his psyche. Including all affective expressions. Interestingly, much of this is an issue in which Anglo-American and Latin American cultures converge, although for very different reasons. It seems appropriate, as we have stated at the beginning of this section, to include all of Indian and Mestizo sectors of these societies, since they all went through the colonial period and everything that it represented. Whether this refers to South American or Central American Indians, they all went through colonial oppression and longing for freedom. In the same way, they all had to repress their desie of rebellion. Therefore, we can say that the Mexican trait of dissimulation is shared by other Latin American nationalities which include a significant Mestizo population. As we said earlier, there is another element, represented by the African migration in a good number of Latin American countries that has given a special identity to the character of such nations. However, Indian ancestry represents a large percentage of Latin America's population and therefore its idiosyncratic traits are present in virtually all of what we call Latin culture. Octavio Paz says that dissimulation becomes mimicry when it is taken to an extreme. Indians blend with landscape, Paz says, with a white wall, dark soil or the silence that surrounds them. They become stone, wall, silence and ultimately space. But mimicry is not just a defense against the outside world; it can also be a fascination with inert matter, with death. It does not really imply a change of nature as much as of appearance. Paz says that it is a question of choosing the appearance of death or of inert space at rest. The Mexican soul prefers the appearance of death to open up its intimacy (p. 39).

In this fashion, mimetic dissimulation is just one of many of Mexicans' manifestations of hermetism. Ocatvio Paz mentions a very common expression in Spanish: "No es nadie. Soy yo", meaning "It's only me", the colloquial counterpart in English (p. 40). Paz says that at least in the eyes of others, there seems to be an inferiority complex in Mexicans, but the reserve presented by the Mexican character has more to do with a cultural loneliness in which he finds himself. This is more evident with Mexicans that live abroad. The history of Mexico is that of the man who looks for his origin and affiliation. Mexico has been Hispanicist, Francophilic, Indigenist, etc. (p 18). Somehow, it strives to go back to the center of the life from which it was detached, whether it happened during the conquest or the independence. The distrust presented by the Mexican character provokes the foreigner's suspicion. His unexpected violence, the solemnity and splendor of his celebrations, his worship of death, all bewilder the foreigner.

Octavio Paz considers the Mexican to have an ambiguous image of his culture, at times contradictory. He says that there is no reliability in his attitude, his responses are like his silence, unpredictable and unexpected. Treachery and loyaltiy, crime and love: they can all be revealed in the depth of his look. His personality attracts and repels. To most foreigners, especially Europeans and Anglo-Americans, Mexico and Latin America are on the fringe of universal history. And everything distant from the center of a particular society appears strange and impenetrable (p.59).

It seems that loneliness is a common denominator of both Anglo-Saxon and Hispanic cultures, although the reasons behind that loneliness are very different in each case. The origin of culturally caused Anlgo-Saxon loneliness is the drive towards self-reliance, which makes the individual strive to become independent in almost every aspect of life. The reason for the culturally based loneliness in Hispanic society is the individual's drive to close ranks within himself, for fear of being exposed, this being a feature of the great sector of Hispanic society composed by the Mestizo and Indian groups. The need to close himself to the world is probably not shared by the peninsular Spanish element of Hispanic culture, but it is not characterized either by the drive towards self-reliance distinctive in Anglo-Saxon culture. Its Arabic, Jewish, and Roman heritage has given the Spanish character a more volatile nature, which has also influenced the Mestizo and Indian character, but in such a way that it does not interfere with the impulse towards inner confinement.

Octavio Paz says: "The solitary Mexican loves parties and public gatherings." There is always a reason to celebrate, whether religious or political. The calendar is crowded with holidays. In all these celebrations Mexicans open up to the exterior. They all give the Mexican personality the opportunity to reveal itself and dialogue with God, the country, the friends or the family, says

Octavio Paz. The otherwise quiet Mexican whistles, yells, sings and shoots his gun, during those days. He discharges his soul. And his yell transforms into fireworks that give foreigners the impression of an ever explosive nature. Later, however, there is a retreat when he has to deal at a more personal level. But when the party is taking place, the friends who during months did not speak to each other, drink together, reveal secrets, cry over their sorrows and get angry at each other. At times, they even kill one another (p. 42-44).

Death is another aspect in which cultures are reflected. That is, the way death is approached. To the Anglo-Saxon, death does not exist. He does not want to have anything to do with it. To the Anglo-Saxon culture, it is sickening to worship and contemplate death. To the Anglo-Saxon mind death can be another barrier to self-reliance. Death represents the one event that binds human beings more closely together, especially those who survive a loved one. This means dependency, the need for comfort and support. It implies the deepest sorrow that is in need of being expressed by means of tears or lamentation. But this all goes against the principle of self-reliance. In a way, to the Anglo-Saxon mind crying might mean losing the battle aganist dependency, because in order to be self-reliant the individual is supposed to shun all emotions, trying in a way to be invulnerable. Funerals are supposed to be as sober as possible in Anglo-Saxon culture, with no visible manifestations of sorrow. But there seems to be a natural need for human dependency, which can lead to psychological conflicts in some cases.

In Hispanic culture, death is seen under a different light. It is confronted face to face, emotionally speaking. Octavio Paz says that Mexicans look at death the same way they look at life (p. 48). They approach it with indifference, wihtout trying to evade its reality and its pain. From another cultural point of view, this might mean indifference to sorrow. However, it is more like acceptance of pain, without any struggle to deny it. And there will be lamentation and mourning, which might look like denial from another point of view. This is not true: there is more denial and rebellion in ignoring death as part of reality. This way we can find another resemblance between both Anglo-Saxon and Hispanic cultures. Anglo-Saxon culture turns its face away from pain. The Hispanic chooses to look at it and accept it, but without struggling, as if it had always been there in the first place. There is a manifestation of the denial of death in Anglo-Saxon culture when people leave the cemetery before the undertaker places the coffin in the grave. There is denial of death when governments play with numbers as they compare nuclear arsenals wihtout fully realizing the reality of their own annihilation.

To Pre-Colombian civilizations the opposition between life and death was not an absolute as it is for modern societies. It was more like the Eastern idea of reincarnation. Life was prolonged after death. It was an infinite cycle. Life, death and resurrection were stages of a cosmic process. When Mexicans wonder what death is, Octavio Paz says, they answer themselves with another question: What do I care about death, if I don't care about life? However, they do not open up to death either. They worship death, celebrate it, cultivate it, hold on to it, but do not surrender to it, the same way they close themselves off from life. Paz says that everything is far away from the Mexican character, everything is alien, including death (p.49-52).

Unlike Anglo-Saxon culture, in which most natural relationships are sometimes considered an obstruction for individuals to fulfill themselves in their independence and self-reliance, in Hispanic culture there are several causes which impel individuals to cultivate these relationships. In the first place, the figure of the Virgin Mary has a preponderant role in Catholic Church, which is not the case in Protestantism. In fact, the figure of the mother of Jesus Christ is considered in Protestant denominations as an effigy that has taken attention away from the main figure of Christ. To Catholicism, the mythic mother figure is sacred (p.76). The mother is the one member who holds the family together. It is probalby more important than the father figure. And it is the mother who usually helps reconcile differences between the father and the children. In general, in Anglo-Saxon culture, the mother is more like just another member of the familiy group, who will work towards helping the offspring achieve their independence. From the beginning of their life, children start being prepared to leave the family nest as soon as they reach their majority. At around the age of eighteen, children are expected to leave and start their own lives. This is literally unheard of in Hispanic countries. It is even considered inhuman to the Hispanic perspective; it may even seem as if children are thrown out of the home. To the Anglo-Saxon mind it is, in the worst of cases, a necessary evil. And apparently it is accepted as the general consensus. Eventually these children also expect their own offspring to go out and confront life, as their parents did with them, thus becoming a cultural cycle. From the Hispanic point of view, the young ones must take care of the old ones. When parents reach old age, they will be taken by their children.

Most differences between Anglo-Saxon and Hispanic cultures seemed to widen further apart when they were transplanted to the New World, especially when the Indian element came into contact with the Spanish and British individualism went a step further and became American self-reliance. As we have seen earlier, Spain received a much more prolonged influence from the Roman Empire than did Great Britain. Later on, it drifted even further from the rest of Europe after the invasion of the Arabs, who stayed in the peninsula seven hundred years, changing Spain's identity forever. In the meanwhile, England had remained culturally bound to Northern Europe where the idea of miscegenation had become almost completely unfamiliar, perhaps due to the geographical isolation of the area.

But even though Spain was subjected to a series of influences throughout its history, it still longs to find an identity. However, as Octavio Paz mentions in his article *Translation: Literature and Literality* (1971), Spain actually consists of a series of Roman, Arabic, Jewish, Celtiberian, and Basque names.

Hispanic culture later added the Indian element which gave it a much more complex and conflictive nature. It also incorporated the African element that has enriched Latin America even more and has been an essential factor in the development of the literary genre called *Realismo Mágico* which has been the source of inspiration for many of the most important Latin American writers like Alejo Carpentier and Gabriel García Márquez, who ultimately won the Nobel Prize of Literature in 1982 for his treatment of reality through a mixture of Spanish, Indian and African perspectives.

2.- Anglo-Saxon Culture

Even though most physical traits of Anglo-Saxon and Mediterranean ethnic groups seem to differ so greatly, according to the historical data on early settlings in Great Britain, there were two groups in the population of the British Islands which are common to the Iberian Peninsula as well, those being the migrations represented by the early Iberian and the Celtic tribes (Barker, pp. 9-24). Of course, these Iberians migrations are speculative, as it is the case in many other ancient anthropological issues.

And there is a further assumption that the predominant racial element of early Great Britain was not that of Saxons but that of the Celtic groups, which, as we have seen, also formed part of the ethnic constituency of the Spanish people. Therefore in the modern ethnic term denominated *Anglo-Saxon* in relation to the making of the population of Great Britain, there was an ingredient resulting from the mixture of ancient Iberian and Celtic tribes (Barker, pp.9-24), which reduces the racial distance between the peoples of both regions. For the same token, both the Anglos and the Visigoths originated in Germany. It seems that the only major ethnic elements distinctive in Anglo-Saxon and Iberian communities were the Arabic an the Jewish, since the Roman component is also present in both cases. From this we can assume that before the arrival of the Moors the inhabitants of both Great Britain and Spain might have shared a rather similar physical appearance. As far as the Basque are concerned, they must have been already part of the mixture of the early Iberian tribes as well as the ethnic contributions made by Greeks, Phoenicians, and the Jewish people. This closeness in early ethnic background does not seem to match the great divergence that later took place in Anglo-Saxon and Hispanic cultures, probably due to the incredible impact the Arabic culture had in the Iberian peninsula, as well as the geographical location of both general cultures.

It seems that Northern European groups, although not unique in the self-conception of a special mission in the world, could manage to preserve their ethnic isolation more succesfully, for geographical reasons. Which was not the case of the Mediterranean region of Europe and the North of Africa. These regions had much more contact between them through migration, warfare, and commerce, by reason of their geographic location and the historical events that took place on their soil because of that contact, like the rise and fall of several empires and societies such as the Egyptian, Greek, Roman and Byzantine; and the spread of the religions of Christianity, Islam and Judaism which took place in that area of the world (Foster, 1960, p.26).

After the discovery of America, even when all the European countries that colonized the New Continent arrived with the idea of a special mission, only some of them seemed more accustomed to the idea of ethnic mixing, although the concept of racial purity was always present (Willems, 1975, p.50). Such was the case of Spaniards and Portuguese, while British colonizers were more reluctant towards and opposed to racial miscegenation. It has been said that the Puritan background of Great Britain is responsible for this fact, but Anglo-Saxon culture might have acquired its Puritan nature from a more prolonged racial seclusion (Barker, 1947, pp. 9-24). Upon the undertaking of the colonization of North America, several of the cultural traits brought to the New Continent by British settlers clashed with the new situations and demands imposed by the freedom and independence inherent to the expansionist nature of colonization. Therefore, cultural contradictions appeared within the transplanted Anglo-Saxon culture which had not existed before the discovery of the New World.

Francis L. K. Hsu

As far as the Anglo-Saxon character is concerned, Francis L. K. Hsu (1972) has made an account of American traits which present (as do their Hispanic counterparts) a series of conflicts, but of a very different nature. Hsu analyzed several studies made about American traits and detected how some of the features that are most typical of American culture represent the source of antagonistic values as well. From a list compiled by Lee Coleman (1941) Hsu finds that values mentioned by Coleman like 'local government' and 'democracy', directly contradict what Coleman describes as 'disregard of law" and 'direct action' . Likewise, Coleman mentions 'equality' and 'freedom', which dissent from 'uniformity' and 'conformity' also included in the list (p.209).

Another attempt to classify a list American values mentioned by Hsu is the one by Robin Williams (1951) in *American Society*. Hsu points out how Williams tries to establish a hierarchy of those values in such a way that the more altruistic traits are found at a higher level on the scale and are more universal like 'impersonal justice', 'democracy', 'equality' and 'freedom'; while values at a lower level are more particularistic or localistic like 'racism', 'ethnic superiority' and certain aspects of nationalism (pp. 210-211). However, Hsu finds these different levels still contradict each other and are difficult to reconcile. Gunnar Myrdal (1944) called the whole issue *An American Dilemma*, when he studied the relations between blacks and whites, and he pointed out the psychological conflict that exists between two extremes of an idealistic equality and a more realistic inequality at several levels of American society (p. 212). According to Hsu, the problem faced by many studies on American Culture (as with those of any other society) is that its scholar-participants can not divorce themselves from the idea that their own culture epitomizes only noble and elevated ideals and that the thought of degrading realities like racism and prejudice tends to be disregarded from their minds (p. 213).

Hsu considers that the failure to acknowledge certain inconsistencies in the value system of a society (in this case American society) leads to a blind spot in the analysis of that culture and clouds the fact that complex societies might show those incongruities as part of a process which eventually can be resolved in a positive manner (p. 213). However, the first step to take is to recognize the situation. Hsu comes to the conclusion that the essence of all incosistencies in American culture is the drive towards self-reliance, which is derived from British individualism (pp. 216-220). However, American self-reliance has evolved even further. While individualism has its roots in political equality, self-reliance extends to all aspects of American Society: economic, social, and political. The concept of self-reliance has taken a specific shape when it is seen in context with society. It seems that American society is willing to go to any extent to fulfill its beliefs regarding self-reliance. But in its pursuit, the social system tumbles into issues that appear to contradict that impulse towards independence.

Hsu points out that while England had adopted a certain form of socialism in spite of its individualism, the United States totally rejects any form of socialistic system, even when the country has established social security, subsidies, and other forms of public assistance. Hsu points out that another manifestation of the greater self-reliance presented by American society in contrast with Great Britain is the fact that the British still maintain royalty as symbolic of their bindings to their past and their heritage, while Americans take the liberty of criticizing their highest officials. And the idea that anyone can be president exists in the folklore of American Culture even if it is not a reality. In American culture, self-reliance applies to all aspects of human relationships. Parents teach their children to be self-reliant from birth, and when parents themselves reach old age they are supposed to be self-reliant likewise, in such a way that they do no expect to be supported by their children, as occurs in other cultures, including the Hispanic society. Under the American cultural system, to be dependent upon one's children represents a disgrace and it is hidden from society if it ever occurs. A dependent character in American society is considered to be an abnormal personality trait (p. 216-220).

However, the whole structure of human society is supposedly based upon the dependency of human beings at several levels of existence. Therefore, when the concept of self-reliance is carried to the extremes, serious psychological conflicts can arise within a community, since it apparently opposes the natural need for human dependency. Often times, the conflict between dependency and self-reliance affects ascribed and achieved relationships. (Ascribed relationships are the ones into which we are born [i.e. family] and achieved relationships the ones we acquire later in life, [i.e. marriage, business partnerships]). The natural bindings that attach members of the human family suffer the restraints that a propensity towards self-reliance imposes on them.

The drive towards self-reliance in the American character is frequently carried to the point of constituting the main priority in people's lives over all the other human needs, including the most basic, like love and attachment, which by nature, again oppose self-reliance itself. Not that human dependency requires total renouncement of self-reliance, but apparently there has to be an equilibrium. The Anglo-Saxon mind can view manifestations of dependency as deplorable or only the subject of poetry, bad popular music or cheap melodrama. Being emotional is an indication of a personality that gets easily attached and therefore it is undesirable to display emotions. Because of this notion, Latin culture appears too emotional to the Anglo-Saxon perspective (p.219).

Body language is another manifestation of emotional states. To the Anglo-Saxon culture the ideal is to minimize body gestures, including facial and hand movements. To this cultural frame, the Latin body language is exaggerated and too explosive. But the American character can not help revealing in many ways the inner struggle between natural human dependency and the drive towards self-reliance.

Another aspect of Anglo-Saxon culture mentioned by Hsu as affected by the drive towards self-reliance in conflicting terms is the value of Christian love, which is in contradiction with what Hsu calls religious bigotry (p.220). Since the foundations of American society rest on Christianity, the concept that of all human beings must love their neighbor is deeply rooted in the Anglo-Saxon mentality. However, that belief is in direct opposition with the impulse towards self-reliance, because this trait implies competition in order to be able to be self-sufficient and therefore, individuals need to consider themselves above the rest of their fellow human beings in order to reach that confidence. One of the several repercussions self-reliance has at this level is the fact that where there is no other religious doctrine which will lead to salvation, antagonism among different creeds appears. Thus, the idea of individual uniqueness is reinforced by the notion of one's embodiment of truth. Consequently, all those who fall outside the individual's range of religious beliefs will invariably be considered inferior and an adversary to his or her own set of values.

Hsu mentions how in countries like the United States, Canada, Australia, Ireland and South Africa there are still religious conflicts between different denominations (p. 225). For example between Protestants and Catholics. Not that these confrontations have not taken place in other areas, like Latin countries for example which have suffered throughout their history repression by religious institutions like the Inquisition. But in Anglo-Saxon societies, religious antagonism sometimes goes a step farther in the form of racial prejudice as a consequence of the belief in ethnic purity (of course, there have been examples of ethnic-religious prejudice in Hispanic societies, as the situation of the Jewish and Arab peoples a few centuries ago). Since, again, the whole concept of self-reliance is based on competition and uniqueness, this is another ramification of that cultural trait. Therefore, racism under this light is the perception that the own ethnic group can rely on itself and that it incorporates all that it is required to be self-reliant and succeed in any human endeavors. This ethnocentricity can lead the individual to consider any kind of racial mixture as unnecessary ot even harmful. And because self-reliance implies competition and this in turn involves a feeling of supremacy, the racist mind regards all others who do not conform to its own ethnic traits, as inferior and unworthy.

Reconciliation between the conflict of Christian love and racism is achieved through the idea that our own ethnic group superiority must be devoted to aid other less gifted and less fortunate societies. However, often times the two concepts of supremacy and condescension frequently intermingle. Then, under the light of Christian love, the ethnocentric attitude can begin as a genuine desire and belief that one's own ethnic group has been conferred with the mission to aid others who in our eyes are not as capable as we are to achieve self-reliance. That feeling can transform into the other notion which demands that in order for us be self-reliant ourselves we must achieve superiority over the rest. All this cultural script represented by the combination of Christian love and racial prejudice can lead to such ethnic situations as the one presented by the former Apartheid system in South Africa. The ruling white minority of South Africa considered that the underprivileged black majority was not capable of governing itself, and that it was the mission of the white South-Africans, (who were self-reliant) to subject the members of other races who could not rely on themselves. However, this protectionsim eventutally transformed into segregation and the idea of miscegenation was considered as lowering the genetic quality of the white ethnic groups, since from this particular ethnic point of view, genetic self-reliance would acquire 'negative' racial traits. In this way, different ethnic groups were kept apart from one another, with the non-white sectors of population living under a less priviledged set of conditions (p. 225-229).

Hsu also mentions as another conflict of values in Anglo-Saxon society the one presented by Puritan ethics and liberated sexual concepts (p. 219). Puritan ethics taught, as its name itself indicates, purity of values and practices. Chastity represented a main point of this morality, since it emanates from Christianity. Marriage was the only acceptable status in which the sexual union could be consumated. However, marriage represents a profound dependency on behalf of both spouses, and it is ideally a lifelong commitment. Obviously, this represents a contradictory force to the Anglo-Saxon philosophy of self-reliance. The divorce rate increases as Anglo-Saxon society becomes more independent. A series of implications are involved in what we have already mentioned as the 'lack of permanency in relationships', as Hsu describes it. Since individuals are supposed to strive for self-sufficiency, it is difficult for them to establish strong ties with their companions. Soon, the strenght required to overcome the normal strains of marriage is depleted by the antagonistic drive towards self-reliance and the union ends in separation. Eventually, the human need of dependency and affection leads the individual to seek new emotional attachments which might result in another dissolution, if the same behavioral conditions persist.

In the sphere of politics, the conflicts brought upon by self-reliance also manifest themselves in several ways. In essence, self-reliance might seem to advocate democracy as the ideal political system, since it embodies equality. But democracy means the government of the people by the people. And that includes all sectors of the population (p. 223). However, we have already seen that because of ethnic divergencies, only the dominant racial group actually rules. Consequently, there will be an imbalance in the democracy of such a society. Equality can not exist in a community where competition is required of the individual in order to achieve self-reliance. For that matter, equality almost becomes a utopian concept, in any kind of political regime. But within the Anglo-Saxon society it becomes a struggle of ideals that manifest themselves at an idiosyncratic level, perhaps in a less socially disruptive way in comparison with other systems characterized by totalitarianism and fascism. It rather represents an inner struggle within individuals to convince themselves that their political system stands for what it was really conceived to be.

Another level of conflict comes about when dealing with other forms of government or other nations. The individual miocrocosmos in which competition and superiority are at the core of the concept of self-reliance, is transformed into a macrocosmos and thus, relations with other countries become strained, as the attitude of condescension and supremacy develop into colonialism and imperialism. For, as much as friendly nations are considered as having the same status of autonomy, there will always be a competitive drive and a tendency to dominate. Thus, a conflict of independence and control in regards to other states appears. Proclamations of democracy and freedom intermingle with philosophies of manifest destinies to deal the world. Ideologies like the Monroe doctrine, which was intended to keep the sovereignity of the Americas, clashed with expansionist tendencies, first within territorial boundaries and later overseas.

In this way we have seen that the main difference between Anglo-Saxon and Hispanic cultures rests upon the drives towards independence and dependence, respectively. From these two forces stem a whole series of traits that shape these two societies.

C.- Cultural Considerations in Different Theories of Translation

In one way or another most theories of translation touch upon the importance of cultural considerations when translating. During the Renaissance, a translator could be executed if he translated a particular word or phrase the *wrong* way, which probably just meant an unacceptable transaltion according to somebody's interests and point of view. After four hundred years the same passions can flare up fired by the notions of patriotism and nationalism which are alive and well nowadays and may even be more so in a century which has seen the proliferation of nuclear weaponry, for better or for worse, to assure and guard the preservation of cultural ways. Thus the power of translation is obvious as an instrument of understanding and communication or as a source of alienation and intolerance.

Gerardo Vázquez Ayora (1978) points out in his article *La traducción de la nueva novela hispanoamericana al inglés* that up until very recently translators constructed their own universe, which they had to justify with a prologue (p. 5). It is also true that translators were well-known figures themselves because they had their own 'style'. If translation is to become more respectable as a discipline, it sould avoid subjectivity as much as possible. The wrong cultural outlook could stand against such goal. There exists in literature the concept of *committed writer*, which defines an author devoted to a cause, usually political. We could appply the same notion to translation except that translation should strive for a commitment which will be exactly the opposite, in other words *uncommitted*. Objectivity in translation might prove to be as difficult to achieve as being committed to a political position by a writer. Usually a political stand requires the recognition and denouncement of the writer's own social reality, which often times implies recognizing a list of negative traits. Being *uncommitted* in translation then, would mean to recognize and accept not just other cultural shortcomings but also our own. The challenge posed to the translator to achieve this uncommitment can be as demanding as the one faced by a committed writer. After all, the translators' task is already delicate and of great reponsibility, and very often they are held liable for problems they may not be at all at fault.

The task of translation has always been the conveyance of a message across different perceptions of reality. However, until recently translation was not regarded that way. According to Octavio Paz (1971), modern man became aware there existed an infinite variety of ways to acknowledge the universe. At that time, translation undertook a much more important role than the one it had previously played. Yet, translators did not have a methodology at their disposal, and much like any other discipline, translation saw many attempts to devise a theory that could successfully transmit information from one vision of the universe to another. There have been those who have concluded it is virtually impossible to find absolute equivalences through translation and that poetry can not be translated but only transmitted through creative transportation of signs. Other approaches consider that the first step to take when translating is to accept the *untranslatability* of a given phrase at a linguistic level, and then to admit the lack of a similar cultural convention in the target language. In *El Libro de las Misiones* Spanish author José Ortega y Gasset (1940) wondered if translation was not a utopian effort (p.141).

Even exact sciences involve difficulty when translated, since there are scientific terms that have no counterpart in all languages, as pointed out by Ortega y Gasset, and he was referring to terminology existing at the beginning of the twentieth century (p.135). He thought there were two kinds of translators, the good utopian and the bad utopian (p. 145). The bad utopians undertake the translation job imagining they can accomplish it. The good utopians on the other hand are aware of the partial success they can achieve when attempting to liberate human beings from the distances that languages and cultures have imposed on them.

Throughout history there has been a preoccupation with discovering the differences among cultures, especially through translation. In *The True Interpreter*, L. G. Kelly (1979) mentions that Saint Augustine made the first study on academic record on translation. Saint Augustine discovered the dichotomy between *significatio* and *sonus* and he also acknowledge the existence of synonyms (p. 8). Saint Augustine dealt in his works with translations of Latin, Hebrew and Greek. All three languages stemming from very different cultures. Saint Augustine must have held different attitudes towards all these three societies. He probably tried to reconcile all three of them which led him to promulgate his well known religious philosophy. However, we can see that Saint Augustine leaned towards the monotheistic aspect of Hebrew culture (pp. 9-10).

Kelly (1979) also mentions the London school which made the assumption of *context of situation*. This rationale included a list of linguistic and philosophical theories that interestingly enough included an approach that measured responses of recipients to interpretation of target languages. Here we can clearly observe how attitudes already played an important role in these methods of translation. Likewise, Kelly talks about superfluous information, which deals with the failure in translation to concur with the source language in spite of the approach used. Once again we detect an attempt to find an aspect which goes beyond the linguistic aspect of translation (pp. 10-11).

Another interesting example of cultural attitudes as mentioned by Kelly has to do with the assumption that French was the most logical, intellectual model for other languages (p. 13). This position represents what later was questioned by Levi-Strauss in regards to ethnocentricity.

Kelly also mentions other attempts made during the twentieth century to approach translation which were more concentrated on the syntactical aspect of the process and less on the cultural or individual factors. These attempts included *volkerpsychologie*, American structuralism, the Firthian approach, and transformational-generative grammar (p.21). Kelly also deals with translation as it relates to its social aspect when he talks about language as an entity that forges human relationships, and on this note he states that the challenge to understand a given message entails the perception of objective and subjective levels, and that the achievement of mutual understanding becomes the satisfactory result of pragmatic assessment (p.26).

In *Translation Studies* Susan Bassnett McGuire (1980) believes that translation belongs in the field of Semiotics, the science that studies systems of signs and structures. However, she considers that the translation process requires a whole range of extralinguistic criteria that goes beyond the transference of meanings (p.13). She also enumerates different perspectives on translation as they have been conceived by various important linguists. One way or the other, all these approaches deal directly or indirectly with the attitudinal aspect of translation. For example, McGuire mentions the idea that language is a guide to social reality and that we human beings find ourselves at the mercy of language, which is the means of expression of the society we live in. In other words, different societies live in different worlds (p. 13).

McGuire also quotes the three kinds of theoretical translation that Roman Jakobson proposes, namely: intralinguistic, interlinguistic, and intersemiotic. Jakobson makes an attempt to clarify different ways to convey perspectives of reality across languages or within one single linguistic code. McGuire mentions that Jakobson forsees the great difficulty involved in recognizing different cultural views of the world and declares that it is almost impossible to find an absolute view of the world and declares that it is almost impossible to find absolute equivalences through translation and that poetic art can not be translated but only transmitted through creative transportation of signs.

In a way, McGuire assesses, it would seem like Jakobson surrenders to the enormous challenge imposed by translation upon the individual who undertakes such discipline. But undoubtedly, a great part of the obstacles in carrying out a translation successfuly lies within the translator's individualistic concepts. In McGuire's opinion, what Jakobson calls interlinguistic transposition is called semiotic transposition by other authors and it is defined as the replacement of signs in a given message by the signs of another code, preserving as closely as possible the invariable information in regards to a given system of reference. This way, the translator must take into account a series of aspects, according to McGuire. Namely, he must accept the untranscribability of the phrase in the source language at a linguistic level. Second, he must accept the lack of a similar cultural convention in the target language. Third, he should consider a range of available phrases in the target language. Fourth, he should take into account the meaning of the phrase in a specific context. And fifth, he must replace in the target language the invariable essence within the original phrase of the source language in regards to the linguistic and cultural contexts. We can perceive in this approach a conflict upon assuming the non-existence of a similar convention in both source and target languages, and the necessity to replace the essence of the original phrase in its cultural context. Thus, we can see how unsolved the cultural issue apprears to be in translation.

McGuire (1980) accounts for Eugene Nida's (1974) distinction of two kind of equivalence: formal and dynamic (p.26). The first one focuses on the message itself, both in form and context. The second one is based on achieving the same relationship between receiver and message. Nida also mentions the problem of divergence of concepts in different languages, which is in direct relation with cultural differences. McGuire cites that Nida mentions an interesting example of cultural divergence found in the Guaica Indian language of Venezuela which does not contain the dichotomy between good and evil, that exists in Western Civilization, but a trichotomy: good, evil and taboo, which seems to place the notion of evil at a slighter better position in regards to the concept of taboo (p.30). In a case like this, the translator will have to assume a position regarding situations which in his culture are totally unacceptable but in another culture are only somewhat repudiated.

McGuire points out that since Roman times there has been a preoccupation with rendering a translation which would preserve the meaning of the original text (p.43). However, controversy over the extralinguistic aspects of translation also arose in earlier historical periods. For example, Saint Jerome's translation of the New Testament was considered heretical because he employed the sense by sense approach (p. 46). Thereafeter the translation of the Bible became a political issue as the Latin language ceased being universal.

McGuire notes that translation turned out to be manipulated as a weapon in socio-political conflicts when different nations started to exist. The transcendence of extralinguistic aspects of Biblical translation was summarized in the Preface to King James Bible of 1611: "Is the kingdom of God words or syllables?" (p.50). McGuire mentions that development of national languages can be traced through the different versions of the Bible. It could be added that particular national interests and cultural approaches must have left their own trademark.

According to accounts of early theories of translation given by McGuire, translators began to advocate a greater freedom in translation, as well as a better understanding of the senses and meanings of source and target languages (p. 52). For example, one of the earliest studies in translation: *La Maniere de Bien Traudire d'une Langue en aultre* was written by Etienne Dolet (1540) (as cited by McGuire, p. 54). He prescribed five principles for the translator: 1) The translator should understand meaning and sense of the original text but he should have the freedom to elucidate meanings. 2) Source and target languages should be perfectly well known by the translator. 3) The translator should be updated in regards to forms of speech. 4) Word by word translation should be avoided. 5) The translator should have the skill to appropriately choose and arrange words to achieve the proper tone.

Another analysis over the problems of translation was

prepared by John Dryden in his preface to Ovid's Epistled (1680) (as cited by McGuire, p. 60). He proposes three fundamental problems of translation. 1) Metaphrase, which implies translating word by word and line by line, from one language into another. 2) Paraphrase, which means translating with latitude or using the Ciceronian sense for a sense view of translation. 3) Imitation, in which the translator can decide whether or not he should stick faithfully to the original.

Alexander Pope and Goethe, during the eighteenth century, began feeling a responsibility towards the reader upon translating. Goethe envisioned future approaches to translation when he said that the translator tries to find a perfect identification between the original language of a text and the receptive language, by means of inventing a new way which blends the uniqueness of the first meaning with forms (p. 64). Goethe also concluded that recognizing deep structures was of foremost importance.

During the Post-Romantic period, it was thought there existed an abstract intermediate language in which all the divergences among different codes would disappear and which would allow the translator to discover the deep meaning in an original text and convey it into the target language (p, 67). In this Post-Romantic attempt we can see there is an assumption that different cultural perspectives can be reconciled and that at the bottom of all cosmogonies there is a common basic outlook of the universe. As much as we would like this to be true, we can not deny that we must first overcome the superficial differences that prevent us from arriving at the understanding that we are all fundamentally alike.

Wolfram Wilss (1982) says that unlike other disciplines which are more systematic like grammar, semantics, etc., translation can not be reduced to an exact methodology. Wilss says that in translation there is an inherent need to make decisions (p.13). Those decisions are necessarily determined not only by the standards of the language and the specific situation but also by the social and cultural values of the translator. Wilss says that in every translation there is an attempt to synchronize the syntactic, lexical, and stylistic systems that govern the *personality* of every language. Such attempt is carried out with several degrees of success. Wilss continues by saying that translation is a form of interlingual communication (p. 15). We can add it is also a form of intersocial and intercultural communication.

According to Wilss (1982) the study of translation should be oriented towards questioning the essence of the languages involved (p. 18). Again, an aspect of key importance to the success of translation is to question the cultures involved, the cultural values, and the attitudes of the translator. Wilss realizes this when he mentions that the very nature of the communication process between different societies precludes the possibility of utilizing a world auxiliary language, which would simplify the international exchange of information. It is to endurance of different national tongues as they strive to maintain their identity (p. 21) that Wilss atributes the partial failure of attempts to utilize artificially constructed languages such as Esperanto and Interlingua.

We could add that the cultural resonances of translation on the individual who undertakes that discipline are also an obstacle for the use of any kind of auxiliary language or machine translation. Such hypothetical devices would have to contain within themselves the knowledge of various cosmogonies and cultural perspectives; a feat that appears all too unreal, as something that would only happen in a science fiction story. It would be the HAL of translation, to compare it to the fictional computer that had a mind of its own in that 'futuristic' novel by Arthur C. Clarke, *2001, A Space Odyssey*. Besides the almost technical impossibility to construct a machine of that sort, another very unlikely aspect to achieve would be the human factor that would play the role of programming the device. Such a program should be ideally devoid of cultural bias and culturally omniscient.

Wilss points out that individual cultural speech communities resist any form of communication which did not develop naturally, regardless of the practicality it might represent. Wilss states it seems political self-awareness and self-respect appear to be esentially important to every nation or ethnic community (p. 23). However, we have seen that it is important to be aware not only of our own vision of the world but also of the others we will deal with when we perform a translation.

When translators disregard cultural and syntactical aspects of source and target languages, they might create a third language, says J. Duff in *The Third Language* (1981) (p.3). In other words, the translator imposes the concepts of one language to another, from which the product will be a linguistic entity, independent of both source and target languages. Duff says translators should be able to decide to what extent they will intervene in order to achieve a coherent translation, which will be structurally as well as culturally sensible to the intended reader (p.9). This way Duff seems to join those who consider the knowledge and awareness of cultural frames of uppermost importance to the transaltion process.

Using Duff's theory of the third language we might say that translators who refuse to accept any aspects of a particular culture out of bias or prejudice might be creating a separate language, world, and reality, which will only be a product of their psychological make up. This is what Gerardo Vázquez Ayora (1978) calls *esperpentos* or *bellas infieles* ("eyesores" or "unfaithful beauties" of translation, respectively) (p.4). in his article *La traducción de la nueva novela latinoamericana al inglés* (1978). Vázquez Ayora talks about the new dignity acquired by the study of traductology and translation criticism (p. 6). He says that traductology and translation criticism are as transcendental as their literary counterparts. Vázquez Ayora points out the literary competence that a translator must have in order to recreate a literary work. In regards to translation criticism the author mentions that there is a tendency to criticize a translation without reference to the original. This way Vázquez Ayora widens the scope of the responsibility created by the exercise of translation (p. 4).

Not only the translator is liable for the production of a

good translation but so is the individual who assesses such work. By saying that the original must be taken into account upon criticizing a translation, Vázquez Ayora is indirectly saying that the translation critic must first be aware and familiar with all structural and cultural aspects of an original text, and secondly with the same elements pertaining to the finished product. Even though Vázquez Ayora deals primarily with different techniques we find that nowadays translations can not only be faithful but also beautiful in regards to accuracy and intellectual meaning. All this thanks to the degree of sophistication reached by the application of traductology.

There exists now a whole arsenal of techniques which were nonexistent only thirty years ago. This is why, up until very recently, translators had to construct their own universe, which they had to justify with a prologue. From his technical point of view, Vázquez Ayora declares that an impartial critique of translation must be an analysis of the techniques employed to produce it (p. 6). To the purely mechanical and structural techniques that Vázquez Ayora refers to, we can add that a series of ethnografic tests could be applied to a translation to find out if it conforms to the correct social and cultural frames. However, as we have said earlier a thorough knowledge of the cultures involved should be imperative to be able to perform such evaluation. And that knowledge must be as much as possible free of cultural subjectivity.

Vázquez Ayora acknowledges that translation and writing go hand in hand, since the absence of image and of the identification effect devalues the text, because the essence of translation resides in ideas and effects, not mere words.

Such a process of identification, says Vázquez Ayora, includes *lexis* or more sophisticated levels of organization (p. 7). In a literary translation, the body of elements of emotional, sensory, and tactical nature, which give cohesion to a specific text, must be detected. Here we can observe that Vázquez Ayora includes the cultural element within his methodology of translation. Among the techniques that Vázquez Ayora mentions we can find adaptation, amplification, compensation, transposition, explicitation, modulation, equivalence, and displacement (pp. 9-11). Except for transposition which involves syntactical processes, all the other techniques require a skill that might be compared with the transmutations that take place in literary figures and which demands to be allowed to figure out the relationships between meaning and form, between message and effects.

Vázquez Ayora states that it is at this point that the detection of thought patterns pertaining to the language-cultures of source and target languages becomes essential. Vázquez Ayora points out that the techniques which actually perform the transmutation of codes from source to target language are modulation and equivalence, both of which are based on translinguistic and poetic concepts of translation (p 10). Likewise, adaptation and compensation are two of the most sophisticated procedures relied upon by translation (p. 11). Through adaptation the translator can capture the cultural essence and meaning of the semantic message. In other words, adaptation means finding an equivalent situation in the target language when there is no exact counterpart to the original situation of the source language.

In *Teoría y práctica de la traducción* by Valentín García Yebra (1982), the author enumerates a series of variables that interact in the process of translation. These are: R-Reality (the universe, an individual's surroundings); C-Comprehension (Interpretation, perception of such reality); E-Expression (Communication of these variables); OL-Original Language (Native Language of the Communicator); TOL-Text in the original language (What is expressed); RL-Receptor Language (Target Language); and RT-Text in Receptor Language (Text which has been translated) (pp. 44-45).

García Yebra tries to approach translation from the point of view of the perception of reality. He says that an original text is in fact only a secondary reflection of reality because the author has been a filter and he/she has imposed his/her interpretation or comprehension on such reality. Therefore a translation of the original text is also a reflection of the first interpretation of reality. He concentrates mainly on sensory preception, be it visual, olfatory, auditive, etc. (p. 46) García Yebra's approach is interesting because he explains the physical variables that intervene in the different visions of the world, which certainly play a very important role in how different societies construct their own cosmogonies, according to their particular experiences with the physical environment, which, as we have seen, is one of the most basic foundations for the development of cultures.

Georges Mounin (1963) is another author who analizes the cultural problems that affect the process of translation. In his book *Theoretical Problems of Translation*, Mounin deals with two opposite points of view of translation. The first one represents the ideas that some texts are untranslatable because of semantic and cultural reasons attributable to different visions of the world as manifested in a language (pp. 17-24). The second point of view states that translation is always possible (pp. 25-34).

Mounin's first point of view refers to the hidden cultural limitations imposed on the translator, which are integrated in a language. The author says that there are linguistic, lexical, and syntactical fossils in all languages that preserve over time, the same meaning for which they were created. Mounin says translators have to become aware of which subjects they will be unable to translate and what their limitations are. However, even if languages have untranslatable elements, Mounin adds, translators must find their way around these obstacles which ultimately means that translation is never inexorably impossible.

In the search for a definition of translation, Mildred Larson (1984) in *Meaning-based Translation* says that the process of translation is basically a change of form (p.4). That is, a particular form of a source language is replaced by another form of a target language. She says that the original meaning must be conveyed in this change of forms, and must remain constant. Therefore, translation includes lexical structure, grammatical structure, and cultural context analysis of the source language in such a way that the same meaning should be attained in the target language. Larson mentions as an example the expression 'I am sleepy' which would adopt different forms in different languages, like Spanish, where we would find 'I have sleep' or in the Aguaruna Indian language of Peru, which would yield 'My sleep lives' (p. 4).

She says the translator must avoid the influence of grammatical forms of the source language over the target language, which is a common mistake. She establishes three characteristics that should be required of a good translation. In the first place, the text should use the natural language of the original code. Secondly, it should contain the same meaning of the source language. And third, it should keep the dynamics of the original (p. 6). In other words, the translation should evoke the same response it does in the source language. Larson says that some aspects of language are implicitly more important to the principles of translation, for example the so called, *semantic components*, which are grouped in lexical or grammatical units, following the most diverse patterns in different languages. That is to say, the *plurality* component can be a suffix in verbs and nouns in some languages like English, or an inseparable part of the verbal stem in languages like the Aguaruna. Some languages possess semantic components that contain several lexical forms. Likewise, one form can be utilized to represent several meanings, depending on the context in which they are found. The same happens with grammatical patterns that can express different connotations. Complete sentences can acquire different semantic functions. For example, a question can be taken as such or it can imply a command or suggestion as in: *Mary, why don't you wash the dishes?* (p. 7).

Larson (1984) explains that one of the aspects that make translation more difficult is the fact that some grammatical and lexical forms can have primary, secondary and figurative meanings. Figurative meanings in special can be culturally charged. Therefore, Larson says, priority must be given to meaning over form in translation. And the goal of translation should be to produce an idiomatic text instead of literal. The reproduction of the natural form in the source language will be attained by idiomatic translation. In idiomatic expressions, words have different meanings together than they do separately. Larson cites examples like: run into debt, fall in love, dive into a book, etc. The author says that in order to arrive at the appropriate transference of meanings, translators must learn to manipulate the mechanical components of a language which should be sacrificed over meaning, which is the essence of translation (p. 11).

Larson says there are two types of information in a text. implicit and explicit. Explicit translation is stated directly in a text, and implicit translation is not stated but is shared by reader and writer. Larson includes some grammatical examples of this situation (p.36). However, at a cultural level this also has a critical importance, since the translator must be able to identify cultural nuances and beyond that, the translator should be willing to respect cultural divergences even if they do not reflect his/her set of values.

Larson says the translator should be able to determine for whom the text is being translated and what the attitudes of those readers will be. This way, translation requires a cultural and social sensitivity at different stages of the process. Larson recommends that before the actual task of translating, texts dealing with the culture and language of the original work should be consulted to gain a better understanding of its content (p. 50).

Eugene A. Nida's work on Bible translating has established him as a specialist of international reputation. He has applied previously unrelated disciplines to translation, such as linguistics and anthroplogy and has seen the need to make adaptations to the scriptures when socio-cultural difference have arisen. Thus, his work has encouraged intercultural enlightenment. He has supported the concept of open-mindedness regarding cultural diversity in order to improve human communication and understanding (following the same line of thought as Boas,

Levi-Strauss and Paz). Nida's approach to translation is based on the idea of the establishment of cultural equivalences in the receptor language and the reconstruction of cognitive frameworks. Some of his major contributions to the field of translation are *Towards a science of translating* (1964); *The theory and practice of translation* (1969); *Language structure and translation* (1975); and *Componential analysis of meaning* (1975). Mildred Larson has based, in great part, her work on propositional analysis on Nida's concepts of componential analysis and semantic structure.

We have thus seen that from the beginning of translation theory and all throughout history there has been a great preoccupation with the understanding of the cultural and social aspects of translation. And we have seen how translators have encountered cultural and linguistic obstacles which get in the way of accurately communicating a given message across different visions of the world. One of the keys to overcome those barriers is cultural open-mindedness and willingness to explore different cosmogonies.

Chapter III

Methodology

Examples of Hypothetical Cultural Considerations in Literary Works.

1.- Robinson Crusoe

In order to exemplify the two cultures we are dealing with, as reflected in texts which have been the object of translation, we will use works representative of the cultural frames at issue. To begin with we will refer to *Robinson Crusoe* by Daniel Defoe (1963 ed.), first published in England in the early eighteenth century. Robinson Crusoe embodies to a great extent the basic cultural notions characteristic of an increasingly industrialized Anglo-Saxon society. The most preponderant trait of British culture seem to be individualism, which we have already mentioned and which later transformed into the more evolved form of American self-reliance. *Twentieth Century Interpretations of Robinson Crusoe*, is a collection of critical essays edited by Frank H. Ellis (1969). The editor mentions in the introduction of this work the independence which is characteristic of the Anglo-Saxon spirit as reflected in the novel's hero who "rebels against his parents' authority to indulge his 'foolish inclination of wandering abroad'" (qtd. in Ellis p.10). Interestingly enough, Defoe calls this chapter *Original Sin* which is again allusive to the conflict existent in Anlgo-Saxon culture between the forces of dependence and freedom. However, it seems that indulgence on "a rash and immoderate desire of rising faster than the nature of things admitted," (qtd. in Ellis p.10) defeats the drive to belong in Robinson Crusoe.

Ellis says that the organizing theme of Robinson Crusoe is the idea of man's isolation as a result of his impulse towards self-sufficiency and independence. But even though Robinson Crusoe deplores his solitude in the island he rationalizes that "man may be properly said, to be alone in the midst of the crowds and hurry of men and business...we love, we hate, we covet, we enjoy all in privacy and solitude." (qtd. in Ellis p.12) We can see this passage as an allegory of the actual feelings towards human isolation in Anglo-Saxon culture, namely, that solitude is not desirable but it is after all an evil inherent to most aspects of human existence, and if man can get more done on his own, then isolation is something positive. When Robinson Crusoe makes that reflection we can also observe at the level of semantics an example of what could be misinterpreted from another cultural frame, in this case from a Hispanic prespective, though the linguistic filter is Spanish. When Crusoe says that 'we covet' in privacy, Defoe is using a term that is not necessarily positive in Spanish language. As a matter of fact the equivalents to the verb 'covet' in Spanish, *ambicionar* or *codiciar* have strong negative connotations of greed and miserliness, and in this single transcription of words we can realize the enormous cultural baggage the translator must be aware of in order to convey the correct message across linguistic codes. In fact, the verbs 'covet' and *codiciar* embody the two opposite cultural perspectives of Anglo-Saxon and Latin societies towards material possessions. From the Anglo-Saxon point of view it can be legitimate to 'covet' something but to the Latin mind *codiciar* is despicable. Of course we can find more benign forms of *codiciar* in Spanish like *añorar* or *anhelar*, which could convey more the cultural validity of 'convey', and there are verbs like 'envy' of 'grudge', which have a more negative connotation.

But returning to the aspect of culturally caused loneliness, and the conflicts that it creates, there is in Robinson Crusoe an inner struggle between 'fear and desire' for human companionship. Robinson Crusoe longs in his solitude for at least "one companion, one fellow-creature" (qtd. in Ellis p.12) and at the same time he experiments fear at "every stump at a distance...'into a man'" (qtd. in Ellis p.12).

This duality is justified as legitimate in Daniel Defoe's novel in several ways. In other words Defoe proves to us that there are enough reasons in the world to be ambivalent towards human proximity. Defoe presents Robinson Crusoe's discovery of cannibals in the island as a justification for the fear he has developed. The "horror... at seeing the shore spread with skulls, hands, feet, and other bones of human bodies" (qtd. in Ellis p.12) shows the ultimate abjectness represented by human proximity. The terror of 'being eaten' by another human being. The fear of being devoured into another human being.

It is interesting to observe the correlation that exists to this respect with religious frames that developed within both cultures. In Catholicism, predominant in Latin societies, the liturgy of communion symbolizes the ingestion of the body of Christ, which is seen as having cannibalistic connotations by some protestant faiths. However, the desire for human companionship is evident in Robinson Crusoe, when he discovers the Spanish wreck and he feels a "strange longing or hankering of Desires... for but one soul sav'd our of this ship" (qtd. in Ellis p.12). And it is also interesting to note how in Robinson Crusoe's situation cultural differences acquire a relativity. In his circumstances it would be preferable for him to discover a Spanish survivor than to remain alone. But it is better for him to remain isolated than having to confront the cannibals.

Also included in *Twentieth Century Interpretations of*

Robinson Crusoe there is an essay by Ian Watt entitled: *Robinson Crusoe, individualism and the novel* (1969). In this essay Watt claims that Robinson Crusoe reduces all human relationships to economic advantage. To Ian Watt, Robinson Crusoe is an embodiment of economic individualism which according to him is a concept much older that the notion of -homo economicus- brought upon by Adam Smith to symbolize individualism in its economic aspect.

Watt says that all of Defoe's heroes "pursue money, which he characteristically called 'the general dominating article in the world'" (qtd. in Ellis p.31), and they pursue it very methodically according to the profit and loss bookkeeping which Max Weber considered to be the distinctive technical feature of modern capitalism. To Watt, the admittance by Robinson Crusoe that his original sin was to have "rebelled against his parents' authority in order to indulge his "foolish inclination of wandering abroad'" (qtd. in Ellis p.10) reflects a transformation in the hierarchy of human values related to the rise of economic individualism. The economic motivation ascends to occupy the main priority of the social order based on individualism. Consequently the "other modes of thought, feeling and action" (qtd. in Ellis p.40) lose preponderance and decay within society's set of values.

Watt says: "The various forms of traditional group relationship, the family, the guild, the village, the sense of nationality all are weakened and so, too, are the claims of non-economic individual achievement and enjoyment, ranging from spiritual salvation to the pleasures of recreation" (qtd. in Ellis p.40).

But as Watt points out there is a constant remainder in Robinson Crusoe that there is something deeply painful, although necessary, in having to leave home and family to better his economic condition. There is "Something fatal in that propensity of nature" (qtd. in Ellis p.41) to abandon everything. To the Latin cultural perspective in may seem unnatural to leave all kinds of familial relationships behind to seek economic wealth. Which does not mean that it is never done in Latin societies, but it is not seen as a 'natural propensity' to the family household. Here we find another example in which the translator could be tempted to be guided by his cultural values. When we look up the word 'nature' in the dictionary, we find that the two basic meanings are 'character' and 'creation' or 'universe'. When Robinson Crusoe says 'propensity of nature', the translator can transcribe it as "propensity of character': *propensión del carácter* or 'natural propensity', meaning a universal trait: *propensión natural.* If he chooses 'natural propensity' he will be deciding for the alternative that makes that 'propensity' a universal feature of the human soul and if he decides for 'propensity of character' he will be electing to say that certain personalitites possess that trait.

Daniel Defoe probably meant to say that it is a universal characteristic of the human spirit to have a proclivity towards adventure and against settling down to business where one is born, because later in the novel he says his original sin was his dissatisfaction with the condition where God and Nature had placed him. If the translator lets his own cultural filter interfere with his interpretation, doing so may lead him to think that what Defoe really meant was that it is only the propensity characteristic of certain human spirits to want to leave their home to seek new horizons. Thus he will be giving a wrong interpretation to the original text.

Ian Watt points out that it is hard for Robinson Crusoe not to see everything through its economic value. In a sequel to the first part of Crusoe's adventures, Robinson goes back to the sea as an islander colonizer. When other colonists that will accompany Crusoe in his new adventures elect wives, Watt cites Crusoe as saying:

> he that drew to choose first... took her that was reckoned the homeliest and eldest of the five, which made mirth enough among the rest... but the fellows considered better that any of them, that it was application and business that they were to expect assistance in as much as anything alse and she proved the best wife of all the parcel. (qtd. in Ellis p.44).

Once again, translators must make a decision as to how they should translate the word 'parcel', since in Spanish, and even in English that term can be taken in several senses. The choice can be especially difficult when trying to decide if the translation should have a commercial, impersonal connotation or a more affective, personal modulation. Taking into account that Crusoe praises application and business as the most desirable traits in the women who will accompany them in the adventure, the more commercial term would probably be the best choice. Thus, between *lote* (lot, parcel) and *grupo*, the more acccurate would be *lote*.

Watt mentions that Robinson Crusoe is a perfect example of the overlapping of religious and material values characteristic of Puritan ethics. The dignity of labor is tied with the highest spiritual values and the mastering of the environment transforms into a quasi-divine achievement according to Ian Watt.

In Robinson Crusoe's preface, Daniel Defoe talks about the issue of solitude, which illustrates the effects of Calvinism in that regard. On talking about how Puritanism insists on the necessity to overcome the world through the individual's own soul, Watt cites Defoe when the latter says: "The business is to get a retired soul" (qtd. in Ellis p.52). Translation of that phrase demands another decision from the translator. Some of the equivalents of 'business' can be *negocio* (commercial deal), *asunto* (issue) or *tarea* (task). Probably the most accurate and closest rendition to the original would be the third one, which conveys more the Calvinist notion of 'enterprise' without totally confining a philosophical issue like the retirement of the soul to a purely commercial matter, although we may never know to what degree of practicality Defoe or Crusoe confined spiritual seclusion.

2.- A Christmas Carol

One century after the publication of Robinson Crusoe another story was published in England which in a way condemned several of the values exalted by British individualism. *A Christmas Carol* by Charles Dickens represented a reaction against the dehumanizing affects of economic individualism. In it, Charles Dickens warns of the loneliness and unhapppiness brought upon by greed and selfishness. *A Christmas Carol* became as successful as *Robinson Crusoe* a century earlier. Such literary success represents in many ways the inner conflict of Anglo-Saxon society over the pursuit of material possessions. From the beginning of the story we observe how Dickens mocks the business world of nineteenth century England and all its impersonality. When he talks about Marley's death he says:

> Scrooge knew he was dead? Of course he did. How could it be otherwise? Scrooge and he were partners for I don't know how many years. Scrooge was his sole executor, his sole administrator, his sole assign, his sole residuary legatee, his sole friend and sole mourner. And even Scrooge was not so dreadfully cut up by the sad event, but that he was an excellent man of business on the very day of the funeral, and solemnised it with an undoubted bargain. (p.2).

From this explanation we can see that the only person Marley had in the world when he died had a mainly business-like relationship with Scrooge. Even though Scrooge and Marley were friends, that aspect of their relationship comes only after all the other associations they shared.

In regards to the translator, he or she has to become aware of this subtlety while being careful not to over-translate the author's irony, especially in words like 'executor'. Two of the equivalents of that term in Spanish are *ejecutor* (executioner) and *albacea* (executor). The translator might be misled by the fact that Scrooge was a pawn broker and decide that *ejecutor* is the best choice. But Dickens probably meant *albacea* since he was referring to monetary jargon. Dickens satirizes materialistic philosophy when he makes Scrooge say:

> "Merry Christmas! what right have you to be merry? what reason have you to be merry? You're poor enough." "Come, then," returned the nephew gaily. "What right have you to be dismal? what reason have you to be morose? You're rich enough." (p.7).

In Scrooge's materialistic mind, there is not only no reason to be happy in poverty but the poor have no right to be merry. However, as his nephew points out to him, according to his own philosophy, he should not be as unhappy as he is since he is rich enough.

When Scrooge receives the visit of Marley's ghost, the pawn broker asks the spirit why he has no rest or peace. Here Dickens uses the word 'business' in a different way that Defoe had used it a century earlier in *Robinson Crusoe*. But the translator has to be aware that upon criticizing the material aspect of individualism Dickens employs a wider range of shades of the word business.

> "But you were always a good man of business, Jacob," faultered Scrooge, who now began to apply this to himself. "Business!" cried the Ghost, wringing its hands again "Mankind was my business. The common welfare was my business; charity, mercy, forbearance, and benevolence, were all my business." (p.33).

Dickens uses the same word, but the Anglo-Saxon reader has to realize that the author wished to convey the overlapping that had taken place between spiritual and economic issues in British individualism. That way, the first 'business' is a financial term, and the second one, uttered by the ghost is a spiritual one. Therefore, upon translating a decision has to be made as to whether the translator should use *negocio* (commercial business) or *empresa*, which can have a wider connotation than just economic. Since in both instances the same word has to be used to follow the original text, electing *empresa* would be the best decision.

When the spirit of Christmas Past takes Scrooge back in time and shows him the scene in which the woman he was going to marry tells him she is leaving him because of his exaggerated love of money, Scrooge laments being torn apart by the two opposite forces of 'dependence' (i.e. poverty) and 'independence' (i.e. wealth). This is the same dilemma that we saw earlier in Robinson Crusoe.

> "This is the even-handed of the world" he said. "There is nothing in which it is so hard as poverty; and there is nothing it professes to condemn with such severity as the pursuit of wealth." (p.65).

An interesting example of Dickens' mastery in transmitting Scrooge's money-inclined mentality reveals itself in the following passage, with the Ghost of Christmas Present:

> "Spirit", said Scrooge submissively, "conduct me where you will. I went forth last night on compulsion and I learnt a lesson, which is working now. To-night if you have aught to teach me, let me profit by it." (p.75).

In Scrooge's mind everything is perceived in terms of economic gain. That is probably why he says the lesson he learned is 'working'. Translation of that word used in such manner in normal circumstances would be *surtiendo efecto*, but in order to transmit the connotation of productivity, the translator should probably use *obrando efecto* since *obrar* carries more the idea of material work in Spanish. Scrooge also uses the word 'profit', which is also clearly financial jargon. The first choice would normally be *beneficiarse*, but in this case the most accurate translation would be *sacar provecho* which conveys more the sense of gain.

3.- The Old Man and The Sea

One century after *A Christmas Carol* was publish and two centuries after *Robinson Crusoe,* Ernest Hemingway wrote *The Old Man and the Sea,* another tale of survival by means of the individual's own resources. In this novel the main character confronts nature represented by the sea and the shark he tries to take ashore. The first sentence of the book establishes the solitude of the fisherman against nature and necessity.

> He was an old man who fished alone in a skiff in the Gulf Stream and he had gone eighty-four days now without taking a fish. (p.9).

The word 'alone' can have the possible meanings of *solo* and *solitario.* The choice that could best convey the setting of the story would be *solitario* which carries better the sense of loneliness later developed in the story, as when he says:

> These were relics of his wife. Once there had been a tinted photograph of his wife on the wall but he had taken it down because it made him too lonely. (p.16).

The aspect of materialism comes up when he tells his young friend:

> "I would like to take the great DiMaggio fishing" the old man said. "They say his father was a fisherman. Maybe he was as poor as we are and would understand" "The great Sisler's father was never poor and he, the father, was playing in the big leagues when he was my age". "When I was your age I was before the mast on a square rigged ship that ran to Africa and I have seen lions on the beaches in the evening." (p.23).

In the boy's eyes the famous baseball player's father is more admirable than DiMaggio because 'he was never poor'. But the old man's reply implies that facing nature is as valuable. The subject of human need for companionship in conflict with necessary solitude shows in the following passage.

> "He did not remember when he had first started to talk aloud when he was by himself... He had probably started to talk aloud, when alone, when the boy had left. But he did not remember. When he and the boy fished together they usually spoke when it was necessary." (p.43).

'By himself' implies more to be with one's own self which would be better translated *consigo mismo*. That expression does not contain the feeling of loneliness, but later on we find once more the acceptance of such sensation.

> "I wish I had the boy." The old man said aloud. "I'm being towed by a fish and I'm the towing bitt." (p. 49).

Even though Hemingway sets his story in a Latin country (i.e. Cuba) he can not help bringing shades of Anglo-Saxon culture in the narration, as when the old man says:

> "No one should be alone in their old age, he thought. But it is unavoidable" (p.53).

In Hispanic culture, it is not considered unavoidable to end up alone in old age, as we have seen earlier. At least not in general. But Hemingway instills in his character the Anglo-Saxon drive to conquer nature on his own.

> "My choice was to go there to find him beyond all people. Beyond all people in the world." (p. 55).

4.- Pedro Páramo

In *Pedro Páramo* by Juan Rulfo (1955) we can find an example of 'Mestizo Culture'. Most of the ingredients present in the make up of Spanish and Indian culture syncretism can be found in texts of this genre. Another example is *Don Segundo Sombra* by Antonio Güiraldes, written at the turn of the century in Argentina.

In *Pedro Páramo* we can observe from the beginning how important it is to the Hispanic mind to have a solid relationship between parents and children, even if the basic conditions for the existence of a family are absent. Juan Preciado goes down to Comala to see his father whom he never met before. His father was Pedro Páramo who abducted women from the surroundings of Comala and would have children with them, taking advantage of the almost absolute power he had over the region.

Here we will find several situations that would be shocking to an Anglo-Saxon reader-translator from his own cultural perspective. In the first place it is hard for the Anglo-Saxon mind to understand that a political system can allow anybody to have such an absolute power without having that individual abide by the law. That is at least the ideal of the Anglo-Saxon political system. In the second place, since the individual is taught from childhood in Anglo-Saxon society that he/she must be independent from parental bindings, it is hard to believe that anybody would go look for his father, especially when the parent never took care of the child and the mother. That way the first two sentences in the novel might not seem to make much sense to an Anglo-Saxon reader.

> "Vine a Comala porque me dijeron que acá vivía mi padre, un tal Pedro Páramo. Mi madre me lo dijo."
> (p.7).

"Un tal Pedro Páramo" might be a source of problems for the translator, because she/he might be tempted to render something like this: 'His name was Pedro Paramo' or 'He was called Pedro Paramo'. However, neither one of those choices would convey the idea that Juan Preciado was not even sure of his father's identity.

An example of the dependence in family ties shows when Juan Preciado says:

"Y de ese modo se me fue formando un mundo alrededor de la esperanza que era aquel señor llamado Pedro Páramo, el marido de mi madre." (p.7).

Another example of familial dependence appears when Juan Preciado talks about him and his mother staying at his aunt's home:

""¿Por qué no regresas con tu marido?", le decía a mi madre.
"- ¿Acaso él ha enviado por mí? No me voy si él no me llama. Vine porque te quería ver. Porque te quería, por eso vine.
"-Lo comprendo. Pero ya va siendo hora de que te vayas.
"-Si consistiera en mí.""(p.20).

In Anglo-Saxon familial relationships, the preceding dialogue would probably be more filled with tension, since after the individual gets married he is usually considered extended family by the siblings and there is no implicit obligation to provide living accomodations for brothers or sisters, at least for long periods of time. That way, it might seem to the Anglo-Saxon translator that Gertrudis' words are harsher than they really are, for example when she says, "Lo comprendo. Pero ya va siendo hora de que te vayas." From the cultural point of view of the Anglo-Saxon translator it might seem more appropriate to render: 'I understand. But it is time for you to go'. This would be different from a first-glance literal translation in the sense that upon saying '... it's almost time for you to go', the actual time to leave could never come, because Gertrudis might never have the courage to ask her sister to actually leave, which is what happens in the story, since in the Hispanic upbringing there is an implicit obligation for the individual to aid his/her siblings, who are considered part of his/her immediate family, even after they are married.

The approach to death is well represented through *Pedro Páramo*. In *A Christmas Carol* we saw how the afterlife receives another treatment in Anglo-Saxon culture. Death is removed from life and it is stylized or horrified. It is not a part of life as in Hispanic culture. The way death is pampered in Latin societies has always shocked the Anglo-Saxon mind. In *Pedro Páramo* the dead intermingle with the living and dwell in the same rooms with them. They go on 'living' after their death.

> "Ahora que estoy muerta me he dado tiempo para pensar y enterarme de todo." (p.51).

In the story, the dead continue their conscious lives in their graves, just as if they were in another room in the house.

> "Tú sabes como hablan raro allá arriba; pero se les entiende. Les quise decir que aquello era sólo mi estómago..." (p.52).

The thought of realizing what goes on around you after death is unbearable to other cultures. In *Pedro Páramo* familiarity with the grave is commonplace.

> "Me enterraron en tu misma sepultura y cupe muy bien en el hueco de tus brazos. Aquí en este rincón donde me tienes ahora. Sólo se me ocurre que debería ser yo la que te tuviera abrazado a ti. ¿Oyes? Allá afuera está lloviendo. No sientes el golpetear de la lluvia?
> -Siento como si alguien caminara sobre nosotros.
> -Ya dejate de miedos. Nadie te puede dar ya miedo. Haz por pensar en cosas agradables porque vamos a

estar mucho tiempo enterrados." (p. 52).

In this passage we can observe not only intimacy with the grave but we can also notice the sarcastic sense with which death is also dealt in Hispanic culture. Death is like a close friend with whom one can take certain liberties and even be irrelevant. Another aspect which is evident in the previous scene is the belief that even after death one needs company one way or the other, and that the spirit will find others to join in the afterlife.

The position of inferiority in which women find themselves in Hispanic society, at least in relation to Anglo-Saxon society, is also exposed in *Pedro Páramo*.

"-Pos que yo era la que le conchavaba las muchachas a Miguelito.
-¿Se las llevabas?
-Algunas veces, sí. En otras nomás se las apalabraba. Y con otras nomás le daba el norte. Usted sabe: la hora en que estaban solas y en que él podía agarrarlas descuidadas.
-¿Fueron muchas?
No quería decir eso; pero le salió la pregunta por costumbre.
-Ya hasta perdí la cuenta. Fueron retemuchas." (p.62).

To the Anglo-Saxon reader the role of women in this fictional community might be hard to understand, but even more so is the fact that they would be willing to participate in the schemes of Pedro Paramo. However the reader-translator has to realize that in the middle of the paragraph it is established that many of the women were abducted against their will. "Usted sabe: la hora en que estaban solas y en que él podía agarrarlas descuidadas."

5- La Casa de Bernarda Alba

In *La Casa de Bernarda Alba* by Federico Garcia Lorca we find an example of the excessive authority parents can have in Hispanic culture, because of the strong dependency from family and society instilled on the individual. We can see in this play that even employees form a paternalistic relationship with their employers.

> "La Poncia: Tirana de todos los que la rodean. Es capaz de sentarse encima de tu corazón y ver como te mueres..." (p. 119).

Bernarda Alba exerts so much influence over her daughters that she even tries to control their emotions. When one of them breaks down over her father's death, Bernarda says:

> "Magdalena, no llores; si quieres llorar te metes debajo de la cama. ¿Me has oído?" (p. 124).

Upon translating this paragraph it is necessary to possess not only a good cultural knowledge but also to be aware of the semantic nuances of what it is being said, since not realizing the circumstances of exaggerated authority could mean misinterpreting semantically aspects like: "...te metes debajo de la cama", concluding it means: '... go and get in bed.' In another scene where a neighbor is trying to comment with Angustias, one of Bernarda's daughters about Pepe el Romano, who everybody knows intends to marry Angustias because of her dowry, Bernarda reacts harshly to the insinuation that anything might be happening out of the reach of her sight. Bernarda then tries to humiliate the neighbor by questioning the reputation of the neighbor's aunt.

> "Muchacha (A Angustias): Pepe el Romano estaba con

los hombres del duelo.
Angustias: Allí estaba.
Bernarda: Estaba su madre. Ella ha visto a su madre.
A Pepe no lo ha visto ella ni yo.
Muchacha: Me pareció...
Bernarda: Quien sí estaba era el viudo de Darajalí.
Muy cerca de tu tía. A ése lo vimos todas." (p. 125).

Anyone not familiar with the idea of total parental authority could miss the whole underlying message of the previous dialogue. Bernarda Alba becomes a symbol of familial bondage characteristic to Latin societies. She represents the extreme form of dependence. In a way, that is an explanation of why Latin societies are a fertile ground for dictatorships and fascism. People themselves in Latin countries expect their governments to have total control over their lives. That is also probably why democracy is hard to establish in Hispanic countries.

On the other hand, in Anglo-Saxon society individual independence prevents their idiosyncracy from conceiving any ideas of 'father government' which will solve all problems for them. The Anglo-Saxon mind does not look to be controlled. The Hispanic mind however seeks more to be guided and led by some paternalistic or matriarchal figure, be it at a familial, working or political level.

But in the same way that excessive independence can create mental conflicts in Anglo-Saxon societies, excessive dependence can have harmful consequences in Hispanic society, as in the case of Bernarda Alba's house.

En ocho años que dure el luto no ha de entrar en esta casa el viento de la calle. Hacemos cuenta que hemos tapiado con ladrillos puertas y ventanas. Así pasó en casa de mi padre y en casa de mi abuelo. (p. 129).

Bernarda Alba speaks to her daughters as if they were enslaved. To a non-connoisseur of Hispanic culture, the preceding monologue might seem more symbolic that real, when in fact it is just the opposite. Bernarda Alba actually intends to isolate her daughters from the exterior world, something which is far more common in Hispanic societies, even in modern times, than would be imagined. This is all due to the influence parents exert on their children, which at the same time originates on the concept of dependency. In Hispanic society everyone depends on everyone else: children on parents, women on men.

> Magdalena: Sé que no me voy a casar. Prefiero llevar sacos al molino. Todo menos estar sentada días y días dentro de esta sala oscura.
> Bernarda: Eso tiene ser mujer.
> Magdalena: Malditas sean las mujeres.
> Bernarda: Aquí se hace lo que yo mando. Ya no puedes ir al cuento a tu padre. Hilo y aguja para las hembras. Látigo y mula para el varón. (p.129).

As we have mentioned before, the young take care of the older members of the family in Hispanic societies. But since everybody depends on somebody else, old people depend on the young ones, and many times they are subject to their tyranny as in the case of Bernarda Alba's mother.

> Voz: Bernarda ¡Déjame salir!
> Bernarda: (En voz alta): ¡Dejadla ya!
> Criada: Me ha costado mucho sujetarla. A pesar de sus ochenta años, tu madre es fuerte como un roble. (p.132).

Kinship dependency in Latin culture, reaching to all levels of the individual's life, also extends to the controlling of affection and sexual relationships of 'dependents'. However, as we have seen in *Pedro Páramo*, there are also hierarchies of dominion. Being the most powerful domineering figure in the region, Pedro Paramo's power allows him to dispose of women at his whim. In the case of Bernarda Alba, she is the controlling figure over the existance of her daughters and their sexual lives as well.

> "Bernarda: ¿Es decente que una mujer de tu clase vaya con el anzuelo detrás de un hombre el día de la misa

de su padre? ¡Contesta! ¿A quién mirabas?" (p.131).

In Anglo-Saxon society each individual is left with responsibility of their own sexuality, at least to a greater extent than in Hispanic society. That is why the concept of family honor is also so different in both societies. In Hispanic culture, the members of a family feel they are responsible and guardian of the other members' honor, much more so than in Anglo-Saxon culture, where each is the protector of his or her own honor. In *The House of Bernarda Alba*, Bernarda epitomizes Hispanic culture's social dependence but taken to the extreme of zealotry. Bernarda becomes a feudalistic figure, who tries to dispose of her daughter's lives, as if they are objects she can manipulate at her whim. In that way she becomes an accomplice to Pepe el Romano's plans to marry Angustias, the oldest daughter, who is actually fifteen years his senior, just because of her inheritance. However, he is actually having an affair with the youngest daughter. Bernarda's oldest servant tries to warn her that it would be better to let things take their natural course, meaning she should allow Adela to marry Pepe el Romano instead of Angustias. However, Bernarda has made up her mind.

> La Poncia: ¿A ti no te parece que Pepe estaría mejor casado con Martirio o..., ¡sí!, con Adela?
> Bernarda: No me parece.
> La Poncia: Adela. ¡Ésa es la verdadera novia del Romano!
> Bernarda: Las cosas no son nunca a gusto nuestro. (p. 171).

When Adela realizes she will never marry Pepe el Romano nor will she be able to be his mistress after Bernarda discovers their affair, she commits suicide, convinced that she will never be able to free herself from Bernarda's tyranny.

6.- La Cándida Eréndira - Un Día de Éstos

In *La cándida Eréndira y su abuela desalmada,*
García Márquez (1972) presents a similar situation. Eréndira
lives under the guardianship of her grandmother. With a
literary style known as 𝕽ealismo 𝕸ágico, which represents
the blending of three cultures, Spanish, Indian and African,
García Márquez tells the story of Eréndira's prostitution by
her grandmother, to repay for the damage brought to the
grandmother's property after a fire ravaged her house.
Eréndira had fallen asleep overcame by fatigue, caused by
the excessive work her grandmother forced her to do.

Even though 𝕽ealismo 𝕸ágico is the product of three
different visions of the world, it resulted in a literary style
with a very distinctive personality. The African and Indian
elements gave 𝕽ealismo 𝕸ágico its magic characteristic. To
the Western civilization mind 𝕽ealismo 𝕸ágico nourishes
itself on exaggeration and unreality. However, we have seen
that different perspectives of the world from our own always
seem unreal, from our point of view.

García Márquez and other Latin American writers like
Alejo Carpentier created an artistic literary form out of that
cultural melange. In regards to translation, translators should
be specially careful when dealing with literary styles like
𝕽ealismo 𝕸ágico which are further removed from their own
cultural experience, because it may be easier to misinterpret.
At the plot level we can observe in Eréndira the same kind
of domineering interrelationship present in *La Casa de
Bernarda Alba*, except for the difference in narrative style.
There is at first a passivity in Eréndira in reaction to her
grandmother's enslavement, which is something that Gabriel
García Márquez can get away with, because it stems from
the idea that children depend on their parents.

In another story by García Márquez (1980) entitled *Un
día de éstos*, we find another example of the paternalistic

dependent nature of Latin society. In this case García Márquez deals with the political side of Hispanic culturally -based dependence. From an Anglo-Saxon prespective it is always hard to understand why political regimes in Latin America tend to be dictatorial or totalitarian. In great part, that tendency has to do with Hispanic individual dependence as we have stated before. In *Un día de éstos* we find the all too common political situation in Hispanic societies of a dictatorial figure who oppresses a small town. The figure of "el alcalde" in *Un día de éstos* resembles very much the character of *Pedro Páramo*, the only difference being that Pedro Paramo did not hold officially a political position in the town of Comala. However, he apparently had the same power over the town we see in *Un día de éstos*. In this story, we see however a shift in dependence and power figure. As it turns out the mayor needs to have a tooth extracted and goes to see the local dentist. However, the dentist is aware of the abuses perpetrated by the mayor in town. As in *Pedro Páramo*, the mayor has been responsible for the death of several people. When he arrives at the dentist office, Don Aurelio Escovar, the dentist, refuses to see him, figuring the mayor should pay somehow for the suffering he has inflicted on the people. When the mayor asks the dentist's son to announce his father he needs a tooth extraction, the dentist sends the child back with the message that he is not there, knowing the mayor is listening to him. The mayor then tries to resort to his power and sends back the boy to tell the dentist that he will shoot him if he does not see him.

Whether or not the mayor will shoot the dentist is probably preceived differently by an Anglo-Saxon and a Hispanic readers. The Anglo-Saxon reader might think that the mayor would not actually shoot the dentist, because his crime would be prosecuted by the law. In other words in an Anglo-Saxon community the town's political leader would never have so much power that he would actually break the law and get away with it, at least not so blatantly.

The Hispanic reader is aware on the other hand that in Hispanic communities, political leaders are granted full authority by their superiors, and even though people are conscious of social injustice, it takes a long time before societies decide to uproot an abusive political system, in part because of the idea that the government is a paternalistic figure and ideally it would be a protector to the people. It seems that with every new political regime there is a renewed hope that the government in power will do what it is 'supposed to do'. That way when his son informs the dentist that if he does not pull the mayor's tooth he will be shot, the dentist knows the mayor means what he is saying.

If there is a cultural detachment, the fact that the dentist refuses to see the mayor may seem unprofessional to the Anlgo-Saxon reader, even with the knowledge of what he has done. To the Anglo-Saxon reader there should be no emotional interference with the dentist's professional activities. However, after the dentist sees the mayor's desperation he feels compassion for him and at the same time he sees a way to become a control and power figure, and at least temporarily, the mayor's welfare depends on the dentist's skills. For a brief period, the dentist becomes the tyrant ant the mayor the victim. *Un día de éstos* represents yet another example of social dependence in Hispanic society.

Chapter IV

Analysis and Evaluation

A.- Analysis Design

In order to isolate and identify translation units that contain cultural issues and concepts I will use the methodology developed by Mildred Larson (1984) in *Meaning-Based Translation* to deconstruct texts into what she calls propositions. After I have isolated the proper translation units I will proceed to evaluate the decisions made by the two published translations of the given literary work and I will try to determine how accurately in my opinion the cultural aspect was taken into consideration.

Larson defines a proposition as a grouping of concepts which embodies a single *event* or *state*. Larson classifies event propositions in three categories: actions, experiences and processes.

Action: Peter went to school.

Experience: I smelled the coffee.

Processes: The sun rose.

State propositions can refer to ownership, naming, identification, location, and description. Propositions have *referential meaning* and *situational meaning*, which accounts for the specific usage of the proposition, be it as a statement, a question, or a command. The elements that can play a part in the formation of a proposition are classified in relations called *case roles*. Namely: the agent, the causer, the affected, the beneficiary, the accompaniment, the resultant, the instrument, the location, the goal, the time, the manner, and the measure. State propositions consist of two main parts, topic and commment and the relation between them. Sometimes relation markers have multiple functions, which must be decoded to determine the meaning of the proposition. Likewise, different languages use different grammatical relation markers to express the same idea. It is also important to determine whether an interrogative sentence are real or rhetorical questions, which usually have a nonquestion meaning. There are other cases of secondary functions which Larson illustrates whith a chart.

Illocutionary force	Grammatical form
1.-Statement	a.Declarative clause
2.-Question	b.Interrogative clause
3.-Command	c.Imperative clause

Negation can also be used as statements and irony is expressed saying exactly the opposite of what is meant. Metaphors and similes should be deconstructed into their basic elements to determine what kind of comparison or identification is made. To analyze similes or metaphors four parts should be determined: topic, image, point of similarity and non-figurative meaning.

i.e. Eyes like stars.

1.-eyes shine.

2.-stars shine.

topic: eyes

image: stars

point of similarity: to shine

There are 'live' and 'dead' metaphors. Dead metaphors are those found in idiomatic constructions. Live metaphors are the invention of authors or speakers to illustrate or teach. Metaphors are very often culturally charged.

To rewrite a text as propositions four steps are followed:

1.-Identify all *events*, *concepts*, and express as verbs.

2.-Identify the *participants*.

3.-Rewrite the sentence with the *events* expressed as verbs, and *participants* made

explicit.

4.-Identify the *relations* between propositions.

Larson elaborates farther step 3.

a. Only the finite form of the verb should be used (if at all possible).

b. The natural topic should be expressed by the subject of the clause. A marked topic should be underlined.

c. Implicit information such as the topic and point of similarity of a simile or metaphor should be stated.

d. Only the primary senses of English words should be used in propositions.

e. All figurative senses, except similes and metaphors, should be expressed in a nonfigurative way.

f. All genitive constructions should have the full meaning made explicit.

g. Embedded propositions should be rewritten as separate proposition in the form of relative clauses.

B.- Cultural Considerations of Published Translations

La Casada Infiel

(Federico García Lorca)

Y que yo me la llevé al río

creyendo que era mozuela,

pero tenía marido.

Fue la noche de Santiago

y casi por compromiso.

Se apagaron los faroles

y se encendieron los grillos...

The following are two published versions of the previous poem translated to English:

The Faithless Wife

(Translator: Robert O'Brien)

And I took her down by the river,

thinking that she was a virgin,

but she was already married.

It was the evening of Santiago

and almost as if by commitment

the street lamps were extinguished

and crickets were starting to glow.

The Unfaithful Wife

(Translator: Ilsa Barea)

And I took her to the river,

Believing her a maid.

But she had a husband

It was the night of Santiago

And almost by obligation.

The street lamps went out

And the crickets lit up.

Propositional rewrite of 'La Casada Infiel'

-Yo la llevé al río

-para tener relaciones íntimas con ella

-yo creía

-(que ella) era soltera

-pero ella tenía marido

-fue la noche de Santiago

-La llevé al río

-casi solamente por una razón

-la razón era demostrar mi hombría

-los faroles fueron apagados

-los grillos comenzaron a cantar.

    The referential meaning of *compromiso* includes both
the notions of "commitment" and "obligation" but under the
given cultural context, the appropriate term would be
"obligation", because in Hispanic culture 'a man' has to
prove his sexual role whenever he is required to do so.

Romance Sonámbulo (Federico García Lorca)

-Compadre, quiero cambiar

mi caballo por su casa,

mi montura por su espejo,

mi cuchillo por su manta.

Compadre, vengo sangrando,

desde los puertos de Cabra.

-Si yo pudiera, mocito,

este trato se cerraba.

Pero yo ya no soy yo,

ni mi casa es ya mi casa.

Somnambulist Ballad

(Translator: Robert O'Brien)

...Friend, let me exchange

my horse for your house,

my saddle for your mirror,

my dagger for your blanket.

Friend, I come here bleeding

from Cabra's mountain passes.

If I were able, youngster,

we might strike a bargain.

But I'm no longer I,

my house is not my house...

Somnambule Ballad

(Translators: J. L. Gili and Stephen Spender)

Friend, I want to change

my horse for your house,

my saddle for your mirror,

my knife for your blanket.

Friend, I come bleeding,

from the harbours of Cabra.

-If I could, young man,

this pact would be sealed.

But I am no more I,

nor is my house now my house...

Propositional rewrite.-

-amigo, yo quiero cambiar mi caballo por su casa,

-yo quiero cambiar, mi montura por su espejo

-quiero cambiar mi cuchillo por su manta.

-amigo, yo vengo

-yo vengo sangrando

-vengo de los puertos de Cabra.

-mocito, si me fuera posible,

```
-hacíamos ese pacto

-pero no es posible

-porque yo no soy la misma persona

-ni esta casa es ya mi casa...
```

The cultural connotation of the expression "ese trato se cerraba", in the specific anecdotic circumstances of the poem, does not imply a commercial exchange but rather an honor issue, which makes "pact" a better choice.

Meciendo

(Gabriela Mistral)

El mar sus millares de olas

    mece, divino.

Oyendo a los mares amantes,

    mezo a mi niño.

El viento errabundo en la noche

    mece a los trigos.

Oyendo a los vientos amantes,

    mezo a mi niño.

Dios Padre sus miles de mundos

    mece sin ruido.

Sintiendo su mano en la sombra,

mezo a mi niño.

Propositional rewrite.-

1.-El mar mueve las olas.

2.-Las olas son millares.

3.-Yo oigo a los mares.

4.-Los mares me parecen madres amantes.

5.-Yo muevo a mi niño como el mar a las olas.

6.-El viento erra vagabundo en la noche.

7.-El viento mueve los trigos.

8.-Yo oigo a los vientos.

9.-Los vientos me parecen madres amantes.

10.-Yo muevo a mi niño como el mar a las olas.

11.-Dios mueve a sus mundos.

12.-Los mundos son miles.

13.-Dios mueve los mundos sin ruido.

14.-Yo siento la mano de mi niño en la oscuridad.

15.-Yo mezo a mi niño.

Rocking

(Translation by Muriel Kittel)

With divine rhythm the ocean

rocks its myriad waves.

Listening to the waters' love,

I rock this child of mine.

The night-wandering wind

rocks the fields of wheat.

Listening to the winds' love,

I rock this child of mine.

Silently God the Father

rocks his numerous worlds.

Feeling his hand in the darkness,

I rock this child of mine.

Rocking

(Translated by Doris Dana)

The sea rocks her thousands of waves.

The sea is divine.

Hearing the loving sea

I rock my son.

The wind wandering by night

rocks the wheat.

Hearing the loving wind

I rock my son.

God, the Father, soundlessly rocks

His thousands of worlds.

Feeling His hand in the shadow

I rock my son.

    The Doris Dana version of this poem entitled "Rocking" omits the word 'child' or 'baby', which in my opinion diminishes the intensity of the Hispanic culturally-charged mother-child love the original poem intends to convey. The repetition of the word sea in the second line causes the poem to lose its rhythm. The Muriel Kittel version tries to capture (more successfully) the poem's general sense of cadence, crucial to the subject.

Por Fin No Hay Nadie

(Pablo Neruda)

Aquí

no hay calle, nadie tiene puertas,

solo con un temblor se abre la arena.

Y se abre todo el mar, todo el silencio,

el espacio con flores amarillas;

se abre el perfume ciego de la tierra

y como no hay caminos

no vendrá nadie, sólo

la soledad que suena

con canto de campana.

Propositional rewrite.-
1.-...la soledad que se identifica
2.-con el sonido de la campana.

At Last There Is No One

(Translation by Alastair Reid)

Here

there is no street, no one has a door.

The sand opens up only to a tremor.

And the whole sea opens, the whole of
silence,

space with its yellow flowers.

The blind perfume of the earth opens,

and since there are no roads,

no one will come, only

solitude sounding

like the singing of a bell.

In The End There Is Nobody

(Translation by **Ben Belitt**)

The street

never was, no one need boast of the doors,

there is only the sand swinging wide, at the tremor.

The whole sea opens up, all the silence,

the space in the yellow of petals,

the blind perfumes of earth open up;

but never a road,

and nothing returns but

the silence that sings

in the bell-metal.

"Por fin no hay nadie" undertakes the concept of "solitude". The translation that renders "the silence that sings in the bell-metal" seems to avoid the word "solitude", which has a more emotional connotation than "silence".

No Es Necesario

(Pablo Neruda)

No es necesario silbar

para estar solo,

para vivir a oscuras.

En plena muchedumbre, a pleno cielo,

nos recordamos a nosotros mismos,

al íntimo, al desnudo,

al único que sabe como crecen sus uñas,

que sabe como se hace su silencio

y sus pobres palabras.

Hay Pedro para todos,

luces, satisfactorias Berenices,

pero, adentro,

debajo de la edad y de la ropa,

aun no tenemos nombre,

somos de otra manera.

No sólo por dormir los ojos se cerraron,

sino para no ver el mismo cielo.

Nos cansamos de pronto

y como si tocaran la campana

para entrar al colegio,

regresamos al pétalo escondido,

al hueso, a la raíz semisecreta

y allí, de pronto, somos,

somos aquello puro y olvidado,

somos lo verdadero

entre los cuatro muros de nuestra única
                              (piel,

entre las dos espadas de vivir y morir.

Propositional rewrite.-

1.-No es necesario silbar

2.-Para estar con uno mismo

3.-Para vivir sin que nadie nos vea...

4.-...Hay un Pedro que todos conocen

5.-Visto bajo la luz

6.-Hay Berenices aceptables para el mundo exterior...

7.-...somos nuestra verdadera esencia

8.-lo que realmente somos dentro de nuestra alma...

It Is Not Necessary

(Translation by Alastair Reid)

It is not necessary to whistle

to be alone,

to live in the dark.

Out in the crowd, under the wide sky,

we remember our separate selves,

the intimate self, the naked self,

the only self who knows how his nails grow,

who knows how his own silence is made

and his own poor words.

There is a public Pedro,

seen in the light, an adequate Berenice,

but inside,

underneath age and clothing,

we still don't have a name,

we are quite different.

Eyes don't close only in order to sleep,

but so as not to see the same sky.

We soon grow tired,

and as if they were sounding the bell

to call us to school,

we return to the hidden flower,

to the bone, the half-hidden root,

and there we suddenly are,

we are pure, forgotten self,

the true being

within the four walls of ouw singular skin,

between the two points of living and dying.

No One Need Whistle

(Translation by Ben Belitt)

No one need whistle

to live to himself

and keep in the shadow.

In the rush of a multitude or th open light of
                                                    (the day

we remember: we think of ourselves,

the nude and the intimate one,

he who knows how his figernails lengthen,

how to order his silences

and contrive his poor speech out of words.

The Pedros live on,

and the lights, and the satisfactory
                              (Berenices,
yet always within us

under the birthdays and clothing

we know ourselves nameless

and call ourselves alien.

Shutting our eyes, we ask more than a habit
                              (of slumber:
we long to efface the identical sky.

And we suddenly tire of it all;

like schoolboys

whom the summoning bell rings indoors,

we go back to the stealth of the petal,

the bone, the half-secret roots-

and then all at once we are there:

the forgotten, the purest in heart,

undissembled,

between four walls of unmatchable skin

and two blades of our living and dying.

In this poem we find the notion of solitude also, which is seen under a different perspective in both cultures. The subject of the poem deals with man's intimate self. In Hispanic culture "estar solo" is less natural than being with other people. "Living to oneself" implies being with people but without revealing one's inner thoughts. "To be alone" means not having anybody around oneself, therefore "to live to himself" is more appropriate.

El Muerto

(Jorge Luis Borges)

For a review of the original of this short story refer to:

Borges, Jorge Luis. "El Muerto". In *El Aleph*. Vol. III of *Obras Completas*. Buenos Aires: Emece Editores, S. A., 1957.

The Dead Man

(Translation by Anthony Kerrigan)

"...Otalora determines to rise to the rank of contrabandist. One night, two comrades are to cross the frontier and bring back a quantity of cane brandy; Otalora picks a quarrel with one of them, wounds him, and then takes his place. He is moved to it by ambition, and also by some dark sense of loyalty. Let that man (he thinks) realize, once and for all, that I'm worth more than all his Uruguayans put together." (p.28)

The Dead Man

(Translation by N. T. di Giovanni)

"...Otalora decides to work himself up to the level of smuggler. One night, as two of his companions are about to go over the border to bring back a consignment of rum, Otalora picks a fight with one of them, wounds him, and takes his place. He is driven by ambition and also by a dim sense of loyalty. The man (he thinks) will come to find out that I'm worth more than all his Uruguayans put together." (p.175)

El Muerto

Propositional Rewrite.-

1.- Sólo ve a Azevedo Bandeira una vez.

2.- Lo ve durante el tiempo del aprendizaje.

3.- Pero lo recuerda muy bien.

4.- Porque trabajar para Bandeira significa ser considerado temido.

5.- Y porque para los gauchos Bandeira puede superar cualquier temeridad.

6.- Alguien cree que nació en Brasil.

7.- Aunque eso podría rebajarlo ante los ojos de los argentinos.

8.- Pero eso contribuye a hacer su personalidad más misteriosa.

9.- Tal hecho hace pensar en selvas populosas, ciénagas, en inextricables y casi infinitas distancias.

10.-Poco a poco Otalora se entera de los negocios de Bandeira.

11.-Se da cuenta que los negocios de Bandeira son múltiples.

12.-Se da cuenta que el primer negocio es el contrabando.

13.-Otalora es tropero.

14.-Ser tropero es ser sirviente.

15.-Otalora se propone ascender a
contrabandista.

16.-Una noche dos de los compañeros
cruzan la frontera.

17.-Vuelven con unas partidas de cañas.

18.-Otalora provoca a uno de ellos.

19.-Otalora lo hiere.

20.-Otalora toma su lugar.

21.-Otalora actúa por ambición.

22.-También actúa por una extraña
fidelidad.

23.-Su intención es (que Bandeira se de
cuenta de algo).

38.-Quiere convencerlo de (que él vale
más que los demás).

The term *ambición* has a negative connotation in Spanish and it means "greed", while in English "ambition" has a positive connotation derived from the notion of legitimately pursuing material wealth. Therefore "greed" would be a more appropriate word in this case.

The Picture of Dorian Gray

(Oscar Wilde)

The following excerpts belong to the first chapter of the novel. They will be presented in the following order:

1.-Quotation of the original.

2.-Propositional rewrite.

3.-Translation by Monserrat Alfau from the Spanish edition by Editorial Porrúa.

4.-Translation edited by Ettore Pierri from the Spanish edition by Editores Unidos Mexicanos.

5.-Analysis.

1.-Quotation: "When I like people immensely I never tell their names to anyone." (p.6)

2.-Propositional rewrite: -When I become

fond of somebody...

3.-Translation: "Cuando amo a alguien apasionadamente, no digo a nadie su nombre. (p.4)

4.-Translation: "Cuando quiero a alguien intensamente, no me gusta decir su nombre a nadie." (p.13)

5.- Analysis: Both *amo* and *quiero* are excessively emotional to describe what Basil tries to convey so far in the dialogue. *Aprecio* would be more appropriate.

1.-Quotation: "You seem to forget that I am married, and the one charm of marriage is that it makes a life of deception absolutely necessary for both parties." (p.6)

2.-Propositional rewrite: -...a life of falseness...

3.-Translation: "Pareces olvidar que estoy casado, y que el único placer de mi matrimonio es que proporciona una vida de farsa completamente necesaria a las dos partes." (p.5)

4.-Translation: "Pareces olvidar que estoy casado y que el único encanto del matrimonio está en que hace absolutamente necesario a ambas partes una vida de superchería." (p.13)

5.-Analysis: *Farsa* would be the correct translation since *superchería* has a referential meaning of "trick" and "illusion" and Basil is referring to "cheating" in marriage.

1.-Quotation: "My wife is very good at it. Much better in fact than I am. She never gets confused over her dates, and I always do. But when she does find me out she makes no row at all. I sometimes wish she would, but she merely laughs at me." (p.7)

2.-Propositional rewrite: -...my wife is very good at lying...

3.-Translation: "En ese orden de ideas, mi mujer se supera. Nunca se enreda en sus citas y yo sí; cuando se da cuenta no se enfada conmigo: muchas veces lo desearía, pero nada más se ríe en mi cara." (p.5)

4.-Translation: "Mi mujer, en este aspecto, es algo extraordinario; en verdad, muy superior a mí. Jamás confunde las fechas, cosa que a mí me ocurre. Pero cuando me descubre algo, no arma ninguna trifulca. A veces me gustaría que las armase; pero no, se limita a reirse de mí." (p.13)

5.- Analysis: The phrase *se supera* has a positive connotation which does not characterize correctly the kind of behavior it is portrayed. The phrase *es algo extraordinario* can have both connotations, and therefore it suits better the situation.

1.-Quotation: "I believe that you are really a very good husband, but that you are thoroughly ashamed of your own virtues. You are an extraordinary fellow.   You never say a moral thing, and you never do a wrong thing. Your cynicism is simply a pose." (p.7)

2.-Propositional rewrite: -you never say a moral thing, but...

3.-Translation: "Te creo un marido buenísimo, avergonzado de tus propias virtudes. Eres un ser verdaderamente extraordinario. No dices nunca una cosa moral ni haces nunca una cosa mala. Tu cinismo es simplemente una pose." (p.5)

4.-Translation: "Creo que eres un buen marido, pero creo también que te avergüenzas de tus propias virtudes. Eres un hombre realmente extraordinario. No dices una sola cosa moral, y jamás haces nada descarriado. Tu cinismo es sencillamente una pose.

5.-Analysis: Instead of *ni* or *y* which makes the phrase confusing to the reader, *pero* would provide a better contrast between both ideas. Otherwise the phrase "you never say a moral thing" appears to have a positive connotation.

1.-Quotation: "You know yourself, Harry how independent I am by nature. I have always been my own master." (p.10)

2.-Propositional rewrite: -I have always been in control of myself...

3.-Translation: "Ya sabes, Harry, lo independiente que es mi naturaleza. Siempre he sido dueño de mí mismo..." (p.6)

4.-Translation: "Tú mismo sabes Harry, que independiente soy por naturaleza. Siempre he sido mi propio dueño..." (p.15)

5.-Analysis: *Dueño de mí mismo* conveys better the idea of an idependent nature. *Mi propio dueño* has a more physical connotation.

1.-Quotation: "Conscience and cowardice are really the same thing Basil. Conscience is the trade-name of the firm. That is all." (p.10)

2.-Propositional rewrite: -Conscience is the identity of the firm.

3.-Translation: "-La conciencia y la cobardía son realmente lo mismo, Basilio. La conciencia no es más que la etiqueta engañosa de la firmeza. Eso es todo." (p.6)

4.-Translation: "-Conciencia y cobardía son en realidad una y la misma cosa, Basil. La conciencia no es más que el nombre comercial de la casa. Eso es todo." (p.15)

5.- Analysis: *Nombre comercial de la casa* overtranslates towards the commercial connotation of "trade mark".

1.-Quotation: "You don't understand what friendship is Harry, he murmured -or what enmity is for that matter. You like every one. That is to say you are indifferent to every one." (p.12)

2.-Propositional rewrite: -you don't understand the concepts of friendship or enmity...

3.-Translation: "-No puedes comprender, Harry -murmuró-, en que clase de amistad o en que clase de odio puede convertirse en este caso particular.   Quieres a todo el mundo, que es como si no quisieras a nadie." (p. 7)

4.-Translation: "-Tú no sabes lo que significa la amistad. Harry, ni la enemistad -murmuró- sobre todo en esta ocasión. Tú quieres a todo el mundo, lo que vale tanto como no querer a nadie." (p.17)

5.-Analysis: The version *No puedes comprender...* missed the ironic meaning of calculated detachment in the original text.

1.-Quotation: "-Oh, brothers! I don't care for brothers. My elder brother won't die, and my younger brothers seem never to do anything else.
-Harry! exclaimed Hallward, frowning.
-My dear fellow, I am not quite serious. But I can't help detesting my relations. (p.13)

2.-Propositional rewrite: -I don't have affection for brothers.

3.-Translation: "- ¡Un hermano!... ¡No me burlo yo poco de los hermanos!... Mi hermano mayor no quiere morirse, y los otros mas pequeños parece que quieren imitarle.

- ¡Harry! -protestó Hallward con tono lastimero.

-Amigo mío, no lo digo del todo en serio. Pero no puedo impedir el detestar a mis parientes." (p.7)

4.-Translation: "- ¡Oh, hermanos! ¡Qué me importan a mí los hermanos! Mi hermano mayor no está dispuesto a morirse y los pequeños parece que nunca han sabido hacer otra cosa.

- ¡Harry! -exclamo Hallward, frunciendo el entrecejo.

-Amigo mío, no hablo completamente en serio. Pero no puedo dejar de detestar a mis parientes." (p.17)

5.-Analysis: In the phrase "No me burlo yo poco de los hermanos" the fact of emotional distance in the familial relationships seems to be absent.

1.-Quotation: "I like persons better than principles, and I like persons with no principles better than anything else in the world." (p.15)

2.-Propositional rewrite: -I like persons
with no scruples...

3.-Translation: "Prefiero las personas a sus
principios, y prefiero, antes que nada del
mundo, a las personas de principios." (p.8)

4.-Translation: "Prefiero las personas a los
principios, sobre todo, las que no tienen
ninguno." (p.18)

5.-Analysis: The phrase y *prefiero, antes que nada del
mundo, a las personas de principios* switched the negative
message of the phrase to a positive one, perhaps because it
missed the cynicism intended.

The Adventures of Tom Sawyer

(Mark Twain)

The following excerpts belong to the second chapter of the novel. They will be presented in the following order:

1.-Quotation of the original.

2.-Propositional rewrite.

3.-Translation by Adolfo de Alba from the Spanish edition by Editorial Purrúa.

4.-Translation edited by Federico Patán from the Spanish edition by Editores Mexicanos Unidos, S. A.

5.-Analysis.

1.-Quotation: "He surveyed the fence, and all gladness left him and a deep melancholy settled down upon his spirit." (p10)

2.-Propositional rewrite: -Having to paint the fence upset him.

3.-Translation: "Le echó una mirada al cerco, y la naturaleza perdió para él toda alegría y una aplastante tristeza cubrió su alma." (p.7)

4.-Translation: "Contemplando la cerca, toda su alegría se desvaneció, para dar lugar a una honda melancolía que se fue apoderando de su espíritu." (p.29)

5.-Analysis: The version *la naturaleza perdió...* overtranslates the term "nature" in detriment of the focus on freedom.

1.-Quotation: "Life to him seemed hollow, and existance but a burden." (p.10)

2.-Propositional rewrite: -Life seemd too difficult.

3.-Translation: "Le pareció que la vida no servía para nada, que no tenía objeto, y que la existencia era una pesadumbre." (p.7)

4.-Translation: "La vida le pareció hueca, y la existencia una carga difícil de soportar." (p.29)

5.-Analysis: *Le pareció que la vida ...* overemphasizes the emotional scorn the author uses in the original.

1.-Quotation: **"He got out his wordly wealth and examined it -bits of toys, marbles, and trash; enough to buy an exchange of work maybe, but not half enough to buy so much as half an hour of pure freedom."** (p.11)

2.-Propositional rewrite: -...but not enough to trade jobs with another boy.

3.-Translation: "Sacó sus 'riquezas' e hizo un breve inventario. Trozos de juguetes, tabas y desperdicios heterogéneos; suficiente, quizás, para lograr un breve cambio de tareas, pero no son bastante para "comprar" media hora de libertad absoluta." (p.8)

4.-Translation: "Sacó de los bolsillos sus valiosas posesiones y comenzó a examinarlas: pedazos de juguetes, piedras y desperdicios; lo bastante para lograr un 'cambio de trabajo', quizá; pero ni la mitad de lo que necesitaba para comprar aunque fuera media hora de libertad." (p.31)

5.-Analysis: The term *intercambio* would be more appropriate than *cambio* because it conveys more the concept of commercial trade intended by the author.

1.-Quotation: "Hello, old chap, you got to work, hey?" (p.12)

2.-Propositional rewirte: -you have to work...

3.-Translation: "- !Hola, compadre! -dijo Ben-. Te obligan a trabajar, ¿eh? (p.8)

4.-Translation: "- ¡Hola, Tom! Tienes que trabajar, ¿eh? (p.32)

5.-Analysis: The idea of *te obligan a trabajar* emphasizes less the idea of having to endure work than the idea of being forced to work, which conveys the notion of dependence.

1.-Quotation: "What do you call work?
-Why, ain't that work?
Tom resumed his whitewashing, and answered carelessly:
-Well, maybe it is and maybe it ain't. All I know is it suits Tom Sawyer." (p.13)

2.-Propositional rewrite: -...it is pleasing to Tom Sawyer.

3.-Translation: "- ¿A qué llamas tu trabajo?
- ¡Vaya! ¿Acaso eso no es trabajo?
Tom prosiguió su blanqueo y respondió distraídamente:
-Bueno; puede que lo sea, y puede que no. Lo único que sé, es que le gusta a Tom Sawyer." (p.8)

4.-Translation: "- ¿A qué llamas trabajar?
-Y... a lo que tú haces.
Tom reanudó su tarea y contestó con aire negligente:
-Bueno, quizá sea y quizá no sea. Lo único que sé es que resulta apropiado para Tom Sawyer." (p.32)

5.-Analysis: the phrase *resulta apropiado para Tom Sawyer* does not convey the intended notion of fondness of work.

1.-Quotation: "No -no -I reckon it wouldn't hardly do, Ben. You see, Aunt Polly's awful particular about this fence- right here on the street, you know- but if it was the back fence I wouldn't mind and she wouldn't. Yes, she's awful particular about this fence; it's got to be done very careful; I reckon there ain't one boy in a thousand, maybe two thousand, that can do it the

way it's got to be done." (p.13)

2.-Propositional rewrite: -She wants the job very well done...
-Nobody has the skill to do this job...

3.-Translation: "-No, no puede ser. Ya ves: tía Polly es muy exigente para esta tapia; si fuera la de atrás del jardín, no me importaría, ni a ella tampoco. No sabes cuanto le preocupa esta tapia. Hay que trabajar con mucho cuidado. Entre mil, y hasta entre dos mil, puede ser que no haya quien pueda blanquearla correctamente." (p.9)

4.-Translation: "-No, no. Es imposible, Ben. Tía Polly es muy exigente con esta cerca que da a la calle. Si se tratara de una cerca cualquiera, no me importaría, ni a ella tampoco. Pero ésta tiene que ser pintada con mucho cuidado. Creo que no hay un muchacho entre mil, quizá entre dos mil, que pueda pintarla en forma debida." (p.32)

5.-Analysis: The version *si se tratara de una cerca cualquiera, no me importaria, ni a ella tampoco* transmits better the idea of competition that Tom Sawyer wants to establish.

1.-Quotation: "By the time Ben was fagged out, Tom had traded the next chance to Billy Fisher for a kite, in good repair; and when he played out, Johnny Miller bought in for a dead rat and a string to swing it with -and so on, and so on, hour after hour." (p.14)

2.-Propositional rewrite: -Tom had exchanged the next chance to Billy for a kite.

3.-Translation: "De manera que, cuando Ben se sintió cansado, Tom había ya vendido el turno siguiente a Billy Fisher por un barrilete en buen uso. Cuando Fisher quedó aniquilado, Johnny Miller compró el puesto por una rata muerta con un cordoncito para hacerla girar, y así siguió hora tras hora." (p.9)

4.-Translation: "Cuando Ben quedó extenuado, Tom ya había cedido el turno a Billy Fisher a cambio de un barrilete; y cuando Billy terminó, Johnny Miller le compró por una rata muerta y un piolín para columpiarla, continuando así el desfile hora tras hora." (p.33)

5.- Analysis: *había vendido* implies better the notion of

commercial trade than *cedido.*

1.-Quotation: "He had had a nice, good, idle time all the while- plenty of company- and the fence had three coats of whitewash on it! If he hadn't run out of whitewash he would have bankrupted every boy in the village." (p.14)

2.-Propositional rewrite: -he would have impoverished every boy...

3.-Translation: "Y entre tanto había pasado una tarde deliciosa, con abundante y grata compañía. ¡Y la tapia tenía tres manos de cal! Si no se le hubiera agotado la lechada, habría hecho declararse en quiebra a todos los muchachos del pueblo." (p.9)

4.-Translation: "Había pasado una tarde descansada, agradable, con bastante compañía, y la cerca tenía ya tres manos de pintura. Si no se la hubiese acabado la pintura, con seguridad que arruinaba a todos los muchachos del pueblo. (p.33)

5.-Analysis: The version *había hecho declararse en quiebra* maintains more the business connotation of the original phrase.

1.-Quotation: "If he had been a great and wise philosopher, like the writer of this book, he would now have comprehended that Work consists of whatever a body is obliged to do, and that Play consists of whatever a body in not obliged to do." **(p.14)**

2.-Propositional rewrite:
-Work represents obligation.
-Pleasure does not represent obligation.

3.-Translation: "Si hubiera sido filósofo, como el autor de este libro, hubiera comprendido entonces que lo que estamos obligados a hacer, es trabajo, sea lo que fuere; y que placer es todo aquello que hacemos porque se nos da la gana." (p.9)

4.-Translation: "Si hubiese sido un agudo y sagaz filósofo como el autor de este libro, habría comprendido que 'trabajo' es todo aquello que el hombre está obligado a hacer, y 'diversión' todo lo que hace por su gusto." (p.34)

5.-Analysis: *Si hubiera sido filósofo...* does not make relevant the notion of work as intended in the original phrase.

Chapter V

Summary and Conclusions

I have dealt is this project with the importance of cross-cultural considerations in translation, specifically in the case of English and Spanish languages. The purpose of the study was to show the necessity of a profound knowledge of the cultural background of the two linguistic codes when the task of translation is attempted.

I have focused on the values and cultural concepts as determined by the developmental circumstances of Anglo-Saxon an Hispanic societies. The understanding of such historical and sociological antecedents is fundamental to any formal study of the nature of a language, be it semantic, structural, syntactical or morphological. Disregarding the cultural milieu of a given language undermines de validity of any further analyses, since structural and technical models of language analysis can not fully predict or unravel the reasons behind the different cultural paths followed by distinctive languages if they are solely based on logical assumptions. In this way, this study did not intend to represent a structural, but rather an anthropological perspective of translation.

In order to obtain a deeper knowledge of Anglo-Saxon and Hispanic cultures I did research on different diciplines dealing with the subject, since it seemed in my opinion that analyses of both societies done by well-known scholars will provide a more scientific understanding of the problem. Although the translator-ethnographer can approach the issue through other means, like sociological surveys in the specific cultural communities.

I gathered a list of fundamental characteristics, essential to the understanding of each culture, based on the sociological and anthropological theories and models which analyze the concept of culture in general, and Anglo-Saxon and Hispanic cultures in particular, represented by the ideas of Boas, Hymes and Lévi-Strauss (at the general level) and Hsu, Williams and Paz (in regards to the actual Anglo-Saxon and Hispanic cultures). I found that there are two predominant traits which shape and are frequently evident over the whole panorama of both Anglo-Saxon and Hispanic cultures. Those two attributes are independence and dependence in Anlgo-Saxon and Hispanic cultures, respectively. These two preeminent characteristics can be traced in most cultural aspects of both systems. Since very often these cultural ramifications are in direct opposition between the two cultures, there exists the danger that the translator overlooks consciously or unconsciously, values that are negative from his cultural point of view. In this way, after identifying the proper cultural traits the translator has to assess them objectively and convey them successfully.

To further illustrate the importance of cultural considerations in translation, I selected a number of literary works from which I identified translation units that might require a certain cultural awareness from the translator. And to provide with an empirical reinforcement for the study, I compared published translations of well known English and Spanish literary works. In order to deconstruct the text to identify and isolate units of translation which contained cultural concepts I employed Mildred Larsen's propositional rewrite methodology.

According to the results I obtained there were evident differences among the translations depending on whether or not they took into account basic cultural issues which meant that some translations conveyed more faithfully the message of the original text.

BIBLIOGRAPHY

BIBLIOGRAPHY

Agar, Michael. *Ethnography and Cognition*. Minneapolis: Burgess Publishing Company, 1974.

Arberry, A. J. *Hafiz and his English Translators*. Islamic Culture 20. 111-128, 229-249. 1946.

Barea, Arturo. *Lorca, the Poet and his People*. Trans. Ilsa Barea. London: Faber and Faber, 1954.

Barker, Ernest. *The Character of England*. Oxford: Oxford University Press: 1947.

Bassnett, Susan. *Translation Studies*. New York: Methuen, 1980.

Boas, Franz. *The Mind of Primitive Man*. New York, 1911.

Borges, J. L. *A Personal Anthology*. Trans. Anthony Kerrigan. New York: Grove Press, Inc., 1967.

_____. "El Muerto" and "Emma Zunz". In *El Aleph*. Vol. III of *Obras Completas*. Buenos Aires: Emece Editores, S. A., 1957.

_____. "Emma Zunz". *In Partisan Review* , Volume XVI, Number 1. Jan. 1949, pp. 937-941.

_____. *Labyrinths*. Ed. Donald A. Yates et al. New York: New Directions Publishing Corporation, 1964.

_____. "The Dead Man". In *Borges, a Reader*. Ed. Emir Rodriguez Monegal et al. Trans. N. T. di Giovanni. New York: E. P. Dutton, 1981.

Brislin, Richard, et al. *Cross-Cultural Research Methods*. New York: John Wiley & Sons, Inc., 1973.

_____. *Translation: Applications and Research*. New York: Gardner Press, 1976.

Case, Charles A. *Culture, The Human Plan: Essays in the Anthropological Interpretation of Human Behavior*. Washington, D. C.: University Press of America, 1977.

Case, Pierre. *Training for the Cross-Cultural Mind*. Washington, D. C.: Sietar, 1980.

Clarke, Arthur C. *2001, A Space Odyssey*. New York: New American Library, 1968.

Cresswell, Robert. *Elements D'Ethnologie*. Paris: Armand

Colin, 1975.

Defoe, Daniel. *Robinson Crusoe*. New York: Dell, 1963.

Dickens, Charles. *A Christmas Carol*. New York: Columbia University Press, 1956.

Duff, J. *The Third Language*. Oxford: Pergamon Press, Ltd., 1981.

Eysenck, H. J. *The I. Q. Argument, Race, Intelligence and Education*. New York: The Library Press, 1971.

Foster, George M. *Culture and Conquest*. Chicago: Quadrangle Books, 1960.

Garcia Marquez, Gabriel. *La Cándida Eréndira y Su Abuela Desalmada* Barcelona: Barral Editores, 1972.

Garcia Lorca, Federico. *An Anthology of Spanish Poetry from Garcilaso to Garcia Lorca, in English Translation with Spanish Originals*. Ed. Angel Flores. Trans. Robert O'Brien. New York: Anchor Books, 1961.

_____. *An Anthology of Spanish Literature in English Translation*. Trans. J. L. Gili. New York: Frederick Ungar Publishing Co., 1958.

_____. "La Casa de Bernarda Alba". In *Obras Completas*. Madrid: Aguilar, S. A. de Ediciones, 1965.

Garcia Yebra, Valentin. *Teoría y Práctica de la Traducción*. Madrid: Gredos, 1982.

Gross, Jonathan, et al. *Measuring Culture, a Paradigm for the Analysis of Social Organization*. New York: Columbia University Press, 1985.

Hague, John, et al. *American Character and Culture in a Changing World, Some Twentieth Century Perspectives*. Westport, Connecticut: Greenwood Press, 1979.

Handlin, Oscar, et al. *American Principles and Issues, The National Purpose*. New York: Holt, Rinehart and Winston, Inc., 1960.

Hatch, Elvin. *Culture and Morality, The Relativity of Values in Anthropology*. New York: Columbia University Press, 1983.

Hemingway, Ernest. *The Old Man and the Sea*. New York: Charles Scribner's Sons, 1952.

Hsu, Francis K., et al. *Psychological Anthropology*. Cambridge, Mass.: Schenkman Publishing Company, 1972.

Hymes, Dell H. "What is Ethnography?" In *Language in Education*. Washington, D.C.: Center for Applied Linguistics, 1980.

Jules, Henry. *Culture Against Man*. New York: Random House, 1963.

Kammen, Michael. *People of Paradox, an Inquiry Concerning the Origins of American Civilization*. New York: Alfred Knopff, 1972.

Kelly, L. *The True Interpreter: A History of Translation Theory and Practice in the West*. Oxford: B. Blackwell, 1979.

Kooreman, Thomas E., et al. *Breves Cuentos Hispanos*. New York: Macmillan Publishing Company, 1966.

Larson, Mildred. *Meaning-Based Translation*. New York: New York University Press, 1984.

Levi-Strauss, Claude. "Race and History". In *Race, Science and Society*. Ed. Leo Kuper. New York: The Unesco Press, 1975.

Labov, William. *The Social Stratification of English in New York City*. Washington, D. C.: Center for Applied Linguistics,

Mcgiffert, Michael, et al. *The Character of Americans, a Book of Readings*. Homewood, Illinois: The Dorsey Press, 1970.

McNall, Edward. *The American Idea of Mission, Concepts of National Purpose and Destiny*. New Jersey: Rotgers University Press, 1957.

Mistral, Gabriela. *An Anthology of Spanish Poetry from Garcilaso to Garcia Lorca in English Translation with Spanish Originals*. Ed. Angel Flores. Trans. Kate Flores and Muriel Kittel. New York: Anchor Books, 1961.

_____. *Selected Poems of Gabriela Mistral*.

Trans. Doris Dana. Joan Daves Agency, New York, N. Y., 1971.

Mitchell, Margaret. *Gone with the Wind*. New York: The Macmillan Company, 1964.

Montagu, Ashley, et al. *Culture and Human Development. Insights into Growing Human*. Englewood Cliffs, N.J.: Prentice-Hall, Inc., 1974.

Moore, Frank W. *Readings in Cross-Cultural Methodology*. New Haven: Hraf Press, 1961.

Mounin, Georges. *Los Problemas Teóricos de la Traducción*. Madrid: Gredos, 1963.

Muensterberger, Warner, et al. *Man and his Culture: Psychoanalytic Anthropology*. New York: Taplinger Publishing Co., Inc., 1970.

Myrdal, Gunnar. *An American Dilemma*. New York, Harper & Brothers, 1944.

Nabokov, Vladimir. *The Art of Translation*. New Repub. 105. 160-162. 1941.

Neruda, Pablo. *A New Decade (Poems: 1958-1967)*. Ed. Ben Belitt. Trans. Ben Belitt and Alastair Reid. New York: Grove Press, Inc., 1969.

_____. *Isla Negra*. Trans. Alastair Reid. New York: Farrar, Straus and Giroux, 1981.

Nida, Eugene. *Componential Analysis of Meaning*. New York: Mouton Publishers, 1975.

_____. *Language Structure and Translation*. Stanford: Stanford University Press, 1975.

_____. *Meaning Across Cultures*. New York: Orbis Books, 1981.

_____. *Signs, Sense, Translation*. Cape Town: National Book Printers, 1984.

_____, et al. *The Theory and Practice of Translation*. Leiden: E. J. Brill, 1974.

_____. *Towards a Science of Translation*. Leiden: Brill, 1964.

O'Brien, Justin. *From French to English*. In Brower, Ed., pp. 78-92, 1959.

Ortega y Gassett, José. *El Libro de las Misiones*. Buenos

Aires: Espasa-Calpe, Argentina, S.A., 1940.

Otterbein, Keith F. *Comparative Cultural Analysis. An Introduction to Anthropology.* New York: Holt, Rinehart and Winston, 1968.

Paz, Octavio. *El Laberinto de la Soledad.* Mexico: Fondo de Cultura Económica, 1980.

_____. *Traducción: Literatura y Literalidad.* Barcelona: Tusquets Ed., 1971.

Richardson, Ken, et al. *Race, Culture and Intelligence.* Harmondsworth, England: Penguin Books Ltd., 1972.

Riesman, David. *The Lonely Crowd, a Study of the Changing American Character.* New Haven: Yale University Press, 1950.

Rulfo, Juan. *Pedro Páramo.* Mexico: Fondo de Cultura Económica, 1969.

Sarana, Gopala. *The Methodology of Anthropology Comparison.* Tucson: The University of Arizona Press, 1975.

Shinn, Roger L., et al. *The Search for Identity, Essays on the American Character.* New York: Harper & Row, 1964.

Slater, Philip. *The Pursuit of Loneliness, American Culture at the Breaking Point.* Boston: Slater, 1970.

Stewart, Edward C. *American Cultural Patterns: A Cross-Cultural Perspectives.* LaGrange Park, Illinois: Intercultural Network, Inc., 1979.

Stocking, George W. *Race, Culture and Evolution. Essays in the History of Anthropology.* New York: The Free Press, 1968.

Taylor, Robert B. *Cultural Ways, a Concise Edition of Introduction to Cultural Anthropology.* Boston: Allyn and Bacon, Inc., 1976.

Twain, Mark. *Las Aventuras de Tom Sawyer.* Ed. Arturo Soto. Mexico: Editorial Porrúa, S. A., 1985.

_____. *Las Aventuras de Tom Sawyer.* Ed. Federico Patán. Mexico: Editores Mexicanos Unidos, 1985.

_____. *The Adventures of Tom Sawyer.* New York:

Harper and Row, 1985.

Tytler, A. F. *Essay on the Principles of Translation*. London: Dent. 1970.

Vázquez Ayora, Gerardo. *Introducción a la Traductología*. Washington D. C.: Georgetown University, 1977.

_____. "La Traducción de la Nueva Novela Latinoamericana al. Inglés". *Babel* No.1, Vol. 24, (1978), pp.4-18.

Von Mering, Otto. *A Grammar of Human Values*. Pennsylvania: University of Pittsburgh Press, 1961.

Watt, Ian. *Twentieth Century Interpretations of Robinson Crusoe*. Ed. Frank H. Ellis. Englewood Cliffs, N.J.: Prentice-Hall, Inc., 1969.

Wilde, Oscar. *El Retrato de Dorian Gray*. Ed. Ettore Perri. Mexico: Editores Mexicanos Unidos, 1985.

_____. *El Retrato de Dorian Gray*. Trans. Monserrat Alfau. Mexico: Editorial Porrúa, S. A., 1986.

_____. *The Picture of Dorian Gray*. London: Dawsons of Pall Mall, 1969.

Willems, Emilio. *Latin American Culture*. New York: Harper & Row, 1975.

Williams, Robin. *American Society, a Sociological Interpretation*. New York: Knopf, 1951.

Wilss, Wolfram. *The Science of Translating*. Tubingen: Gunter Narr Verlag, 1982.

Worcester, Donald E. and Schaeffer, Wendell G. *The Growth and Culture of Latin America*. New York: Oxford University Press, 1956.

INDEX